# The Gardens of Ireland

. . . . . . . . . . . . . . .

Photographs by Michael George
Text by Patrick Bowe

# The Gardens of Ireland

A New York Graphic Society Book
Little, Brown and Company • Boston

*To Patrick and Jane Grove Annesley*

Photographs Copyright © 1986 by Michael George
Text Copyright © 1986 by Patrick Bowe

FIRST EDITION

New York Graphic Society Books
are published by Little, Brown and Company
*Published simultaneously in Canada
by Little, Brown & Company (Canada) Limited*

PRINTED IN ITALY

Library of Congress Cataloging-in-Publication Data

George, Michael, 1943–
The gardens of Ireland.

"A New York Graphic Society book."
Includes index.
1. Gardens — Ireland.   2. Gardens — Ireland —
Pictorial works.   I. Bowe, Patrick.   II. Title.
SB466.I65G46   1986     712'.09415     86-10372
ISBN 0-8212-1619-8

Illustrations

page 1: Hybrid Japanese azaleas mingle with native bluebells.
page 2: Looking across the lake at Glenveagh.
page 5: *Magnolia x wiesneri*, Mount Usher.
page 6: A wheelbarrow seat of eighteenth-century
design can be trundled about at Mount Congreve.

# Acknowledgments

The authors are grateful to all those who shared their knowledge, resources, and hospitality in the preparation of this book, especially the following: Aer Lingus, An Taisce, John Anderson, Mr. and Mrs. Patrick Grove Annesley, Lord and Lady Ardee, Count and Countess Gunnar Bernstorff, The Honorable David Bigham, Evelyn Booth, Bord Failte, Dr. Nicola Gordon Bowe, the Baron and Baroness de Breffny, Mr. and Mrs. Seamus Browne, Ailbhe Butler, Grace Carroll, Mr. and Mrs. Ambrose Congreve, Mr. and Mrs. John Corcoran, Stuart L. Craig, Jr., Geraldine Critchley, Professor Anne Crookshank, Mrs. Jerry Daly, David Dunlop, Cormac Foley, The Forest Service for Northern Ireland, Mary Forrest, Dudley P. Frasier, Frances-Jane French, James Galton, Lydia Galton, Mary Grant, John Hair, Christina Holz, Peter Howe, Brigadier and Mrs. W. S. Hickie, Ann James, Madeleine Jay, Timothy S. Jensen, Esq., Dick Kagan, James Larkin, Barbara Lish, Pamela Lord, Michael A. Lynch, Michael S. Maiden, Heidi L. Marer, David Markus, William Maxwell, Tod Mori, George Mott, Richard A. Murphy, Rory Murphy, Mr. and Mrs. William A. Murphy, Mr. and Mrs. Arthur Muschenheim, The National Parks and Monuments Service of the Office of Public Works, The National Trust in Northern Ireland, Annabel Nichols, Adams H. Nickerson, Cynthia O'Connor, Sean O'Criadain, Simon O'Hanlon, Kieran O'Keeffe, Finbar O'Sullivan, Olympus Corporation, Denise Otis, Mr. and Mrs. Freddie Pedersen, Mr. and Mrs. David Price, Jim Reynolds, Jeff Richey, Elizabeth Barlow Rogers, James H. Roper, the Earl and Countess of Rosse, Ann M. Schumacher, David Scott, Clifford Selbert Design, Harvey Simmonds, Mr. and Mrs. Ralph Slazenger, Marcia Thompson, Norman Owen Tomalin, University College, Cork, Mr. and Mrs. Nesbit Waddington, Robert Walker, Sally Walker, Jacky Ward, Jesse Wilkes, Gabrielle Winkel.

# The Gardens

· · · · · · · · · · · · · · · · ·

# Introduction

· · · · · · · · · · · · · · · · · ·

Irish gardens, like Irish people, are just a little wild. It's the moisture in the air. Plants grow so quickly that they outstrip any human effort to keep them in place. Even when a gardener sets out with the notion of making a formal design, the untamable growth of his plants soon overwhelms it. In the gardens of the French, Nature is tamed by Art, but in the gardens of the Irish, Nature reigns supreme.

Driving along the west coast of Ireland, you cannot help noticing that the rocks and stone gate pillars are covered with a golden lichen—a sure indicator of pure air. But it is not only the purity of air that pushes the plants into growth, it is also its moistness and mildness. Ireland is

At Ilnacullin (County Cork), the native gorse with its chrome-yellow flowers, sea pinks, and golden lichens makes a natural garden on the blue shale rock in May. Scots and maritime pine have been planted as shelter against seaborne gales.

Preceding pages:
Blue ceanothus *dominates this view of the lily pond garden at Malahide Castle (County Dublin).*

The wisteria-clad pergola at Killineer. The urns and formal beds are filled with orange wallflowers in spring, and in summer by scarlet pelargoniums.

an island encircled by warm waters. They are heated by the Gulf Stream, flowing across the Atlantic from the Caribbean. With a few honorable exceptions, such as Birr, all of the great Irish gardens are situated within miles of the sea and so are able to enjoy to the full the benefits of a mild, oceanic climate. In them one may see magnificent growths of rare, exotic, and subtropical plants. No art can tame it, but on the other hand, no art could ensure it.

The west, where many of the gardens are situated, is a natural garden in itself. In May, the hills are covered with golden gorse; later, they are purple with heather. In June, the woodlands are mauve with rhododendron. In summer, the roadside hedges are flush with fuchsia and veronica, the ditches fill with montbretia, and the cottages are ringed with the flowering spikes of Australian flax. The coastline, much buffeted by Atlantic seas, is indented with natural loughs and sheltered harbors—sea and land intermingle.

Dramatic landscape provides a backdrop to many of Ireland's gardens. Violet-blue mountains form the outer frame to the gardens of Derreen. The Bay of Glengariff, stippled with islands, is the setting of the island garden at Ilnacullin. The Sugar Loaf Mountain is the focus of the garden at Powerscourt. Even modern gardens have a similar character. Berkeley Forest and Ballymaglasson have views to distant mountains. Kilmokea focuses on a deep sea estuary, Slevyre on one of Ireland's largest lakes, and the garden at Butterstream is dictated in design by the stream that gives it its name.

The few Irish gardens that do not have dramatic landscape settings turn in on themselves and focus on their houses or on a river running through them. The houses come in a variety of styles, from the ancient castles at Birr Castle demesne and the Talbot Botanic Garden at Malahide Castle, to the holiday cottage at Mount Usher. Characteristic of the country is the river garden with its artfully contrived cascades and elegantly engineered bridges. At Annes Grove, for example, the gentle river Awbeg flows through the garden. The Vartrey forms the axis of Mount Usher gardens and the fast-flowing Camcor is an essential feature at Birr.

Lord Molesworth, who was making a garden near Dublin over two hundred and fifty years ago, wrote to a friend: "I have melons now bigger than my fist in pretty plenty, but my hedges and greens are not near so well clipped. . . ." The same could be written by almost every Irish gardener today. It is our wild style, but our gardens are not altogether formless. Plants are chosen for their individual qualities of color, habit, and texture and are then allowed to grow unhindered by the shears. We don't strive after artificial effects and don't set a great store by statuary or ornamental features. Indeed, Joseph Cooper Walker, an early historian of Irish gardening, complained of the use of them when he was writing in 1790: "Thus, did our ancestors, governed by the false taste which they imbibed from the English, disfigure with unsuitable ornaments, the simple garb of nature."

The idea of the natural garden had to wait until 1870 to be put down on paper.

*The lower lawn at Berkeley Forest (County Wexford), bounded by a hedge of the white rugosa rose 'Blanc Double de Coubert', offers a panorama of park and mountain.*

William Robinson, an Irishman of volcanic nature and explosive fervor, published a book called *The Wild Garden*. He castigated the fashionable Victorian garden in which everything was so well kept and clipped that nature was discounted. He wished to reintroduce natural lines and shapes into the planning of gardens and to grow exciting and rare plants in a lush setting of wild trees and flowers. His was a revolution against a formality that was threatening to stifle. He wished to see the exotic and the common mixing in happy abandon. This mixture has always been a characteristic of Irish life as much as of Irish gardens. At Birr Castle, you can see a rare Chinese lime, one of only a few in cultivation in the world, but it is not grown on a close-cut lawn as you might find in a botanical garden, but surrounded by a wealth of native Irish wildflowers and meadow grasses.

Trees and shrubs form the backbone of the wild garden, but flowers are not neglected in Irish gardens. In fact their use there has a curious history that may need explaining. At first, they were grown in walled courtyards around a house. Then in the eighteenth century, they were locked up in a walled garden at some distance from the house. In Victorian times people fell to digging flower beds in front of the house again. In many gardens, however, such as that of Beaulieu, this "modernization" never took place. Elsewhere the older tradition has been deliberately revived: in 1957, Henry McIlhenny created a walled garden for fruit, flowers, and vegetables at Glenveagh Castle. And even more recently, Brigadier and

*The garden at Rowallane (County Down), made by Hugh Armytage Moore, is now headquarters of the National Trust in Northern Ireland. Here, purple smoketree, deeper purple barberry, and pink spikes of snakeweed illustrate the close and intricate planting of the natural rock crevices.*

Mrs. Hickie made a similar but smaller garden at Slevyre. The Irish rose garden is usually situated within the same walls, although at Leixlip Castle the roses are not grown in the usual formal arrangement but, amusingly, in the manner in which a dinner table might be arranged. Will the 'Duchesse de Montebello' be happy next to 'Cardinal de Richelieu'? And will the beautiful 'Sarah van Fleet' enjoy the company of 'General Schablikine'?

The gardeners of Ireland have a catholic taste in plants—not for them the classical restraint of the continental European garden. They are helped, as we have noted, by the climate, which, like the Irish character, is a hospitable one—it will entertain plants from many parts of the world, enabling them to settle down and flourish as well as, if not better than, at home. So, our lawns are littered with the fallen capsules of Australian eucalyptus, balmy days are redolent with the perfume of cordyline palms (dracaenas), the spring scents of azara recall the rain forests of Chile, and primulas stain the gullies gold as they do in the wet uplands of the Himalayas.

About half the gardens in this book are heritage gardens. However, it is our purpose not only to memorialize the great historic gardens of Ireland, but also to show that the tradition of gardening is alive and well. While many of Ireland's great gardens have been lost, it is encouraging to find that the future of several—Mount Stewart, Ilnacullin, Glenveagh—is assured (by means of state or other pub-

*Designed by Kathleen Levie, a local garden architect, in the 1920s, a circular lily pool at Combermere (County Cork) fronts double herbaceous borders focusing on a beech tree on a terrace at the end.*

lic support). At Annes Grove, Birr, and Killruddery, hard-working, enterprising young couples who have inherited the responsibility for maintaining these gardens are investing considerable effort in them.

In addition, new gardens that maintain the Irish tradition of rich planting in a natural style have been made. They range from the enormous garden of over one hundred acres being created at Mount Congreve by Mr. Ambrose Congreve to the smaller but still extensive gardens laid out at Fernhill by Mrs. Sally Walker and her late husband, Ralph, to the tiny pocket handkerchief of a garden made by a botanist, Miss Evelyn Booth, at Lucy's Wood.

The gardens described in this book have been chosen partly for their general interest for the visitor to Ireland, and also for some feature of planting and design that might provide ideas for the reader with a smaller garden to develop. There are, however, other important gardens that must be kept in mind. There are the specialist botanic gardens of Glasnevin and Trinity College, Dublin. There are also the collections, or arboreta, such as those at Castlewellan (County Down), Emo Court (County Laois), and Fota (County Cork). The arboretum at Castlewellan was begun by the Annesley family about 1870 and is now administered by the Forest Service for Northern Ireland. At Emo Court the magnificent trees are now being supplemented by large-scale plantings of smaller trees and shrubs. Fota contains trees and shrubs from every continent, demonstrating the hospitality of the Irish

*The walled garden at Castlewellan (County Down) with clipped Irish yews.*

*Fota (County Cork): rhubarb-red stalks of* Beschorneria yuccoides, *a native of Mexico, and (opposite) old rhododendron arboreum hybrids.*

*Overleaf: Mount Congreve*

climate. Most important for the tree enthusiast is the John F. Kennedy Park (County Wexford). This national arboretum was established as a memorial to the late president of the United States on a site close to the old Kennedy family home. Further fascinating examples of the wild garden of trees and shrubs so characteristic of Ireland, in addition to those represented in the book, are Rowallane (County Down) and Creagh (County Cork). There are also many gardens that are primarily interesting as the setting of historic houses. Examples of these are Castle Ward (County Down), Bantry House (County Cork), Florence Court (County Fermanagh), and Lismore Castle (County Waterford).

Now that the natural environment is under its greatest threat, gardeners can contribute more than ever to its conservation. Their gardens can act as reservoirs of plants threatened in the wild. More generally they can help people to a greater appreciation of the natural world. Much toward these goals can be learned from the Irish garden with its careful attention to soil and climate, its sympathetic accord with the surrounding landscape, and its understanding of, and harmony with, nature.

# The Gardens
· · · · · · · · · · · · · ·

*The Gardens of Ireland*

# Annes Grove

. . . . . . . . . . . . . . . . . .

COUNTY CORK
Mr. and Mrs. Patrick Grove Annesley

How to conserve a garden which in living memory had eight gardeners and now has only three? This is the problem facing Patrick Grove Annesley in conserving his grandfather's garden at Annes Grove, County Cork.

Annes Grove has been in the Grove Annesley family since 1628. (It got its name from the elision of the surnames.) The house is a tall, early eighteenth-century structure with sunken service courtyards on either side. It is surrounded by parkland in the usual eighteenth-century style. Thick belts of beech enclose it and isolated specimens and clumps of beech, oak, chestnut, and lime provide focal points from the interior.

*Orange Peruvian lilies,* Alstroemeria aurantiaca, *are allowed to spread into pale pink foxgloves and astilbes to give an informal cottage-style planting in the shade of a cherry tree.*

*Preceding pages:*
*The variegated archangel,* Lamiastrum galeobdolon *'Variegatum', a suitable ground cover for a wild garden in the shade, here flanks the path leading down to the river garden.*

*The house dates from the early eighteenth century.*

In the tradition of Victorian times, conifers were added, particularly along the drive, where they now cast a gloomy shade. A castellated gate lodge designed by Ireland's only Pre-Raphaelite architect, Benjamin Woodward, almost certainly his first commission, was built in 1854 to give access to the Dublin road. A walled garden for growing fruit, vegetables, and flowers was hidden behind trees to one side. Here was a walk bordered with box-hedged beds, and a grassy mound, or "mount," on which some Victorian ladies of the family had a summerhouse built. They decorated the summerhouse with ornamental twigwork, a craft that today has almost died out.

This was the property that Richard Grove Annesley inherited in 1900. Working over sixty years, until his death in 1966, he created one of the major gardens of Ireland. It is divided into three linked areas: the walled garden, the woodland garden, and the water garden.

Even early in this century the walled garden no longer needed to fulfill its original function of providing vegetable produce on a large scale, and so a significant part of it could be turned over to ornamental horticulture. Mr. Grove Annesley set down the greater part of it to lawns and borders. From the gate near the house a path had always run between box-hedged beds and rows of Irish yews straight across to the greenhouses. So far it was the traditional Irish kitchen garden. Mr. Grove Annesley, however, laid out a second path crossing the first and focusing

on the Victorian summerhouse. Paving it in local stone and planting yew hedges behind, he developed what has become one of the few remaining double herbaceous borders in the country. Herbaceous plants mature quickly and can be changed easily, or old plants die and are replaced with newly obtained species, so the planting in a herbaceous border does not usually remain static. However, many plants in the border at Annes Grove have been there from the early days. This gives an unusually old and settled appearance to the borders. There are many tall plants that require staking. Oriental poppies, plume poppies, globe thistles, and thalictrum reach four or five feet and give one the impression of walking through a shoulder-high field of flowers. The climbing nasturtium brightens the yew hedges with scarlet flowers. A pair of tall Lawson cypress 'Erecta Viridis' at the end of the path to the summerhouse cleverly conceals the fact that the building is off center.

To replace the lines of vegetables and fruit that grew in the borders under the walls, Mr. Grove Annesley arranged separate borders of delphiniums, Michaelmas daisies, agapanthus, and daylilies, together with mixed borders of roses, ceanothus, and brooms. Across one of the lawns he erected a rustic pergola now weighed down with honeysuckle, rambling roses, clematis, and autumn-coloring vines. In a hidden enclosure he laid out a masterly landscape in miniature: the centerpiece is a serpentine pool, its horizontal line broken by the weeping silver birch planted alongside it. The pool is edged with a thick fringe of hosta, rodgersia, bergenia,

*When cherry blossom blows, it litters the lawns and ribbon beds of the walled garden as if it were with pink snow.*

*Mixed petunias in the ribbon beds, hybrid teas in the rose beds, and tall perennials in the border provide a riot of random color in contrast to the carefully controlled color of the rest of the garden.*

*Opposite page:*
*The double herbaceous borders lead to a gate in the wall with a heavy growth of the large-leaved vine* Vitis coignetiae. *The flat heads of yellow yarrow and the bronze flowers of the American sneezeweed,* Helenium autumnale *'Moorheim Beauty', contrast with the ivory spikes of goat's beard and the funnellike flowers of evening primrose in the border on the right.*

astilbe, and iris, and a miniature rock garden is at one end. Now most of the alpines are gone, but the conifers, originally planted as dwarf specimens, have been allowed to spread to cover the whole rock garden. Many large gardens have smaller, more intimate areas that can act as models for smaller gardens. For a small water and rock garden, I can think of no better model than this part of Annes Grove.

Behind the house is a limestone gorge of dramatic outline and form. The drive from the Dublin road was built along the near rim, its route designed to take maximum advantage of the views of the woodland and gorge below. In the 1920s, a vein of acid soil was discovered along this drive and Richard Grove Annesley realized that he could grow rhododendrons, camellias, and other ericaceous plants that his otherwise limy soil had hitherto precluded. Attracted first by their color, he began to plant showy Victorian rhododendron hybrids like the *R. x russellianum* 'Cornish Red' and those bred by the English nursery Waterers. Then, encouraged by Sir Frederick Moore, recently retired as director of the Botanic Gardens at Glasnevin, Dublin, he began also to plant wild species. It was the time of the great plant hunters—Wilson, Sargent, Forrest, and Kingdon Ward—who ventured into the interior of China and the Himalayas to bring back the wonderful, as yet undiscovered plants, that grew in these regions. Kingdon Ward in 1924 was making up a syndicate of garden owners and directors to finance the first of his many expeditions to the Himalayas. Richard Grove Annesley subscribed.

*Annes Grove*

*Spring sunshine illuminates a bridge of light construction crossing the river and glistens on the leaves of willows, poplars, and gunnera by the water's edge.*

*Opposite:*
*The soaring spires of Lawson cypress provide a dramatic backdrop to the river garden. By the white waters of the weir a native hawthorn is in flower.*

Like many subscribers, he must have eagerly awaited his share of the seed that Kingdon Ward would bring back from these remote regions. In the meantime, Ward sent reports of his progress. One of these, still at Annes Grove, sent the bad news of the murder of his mail runner; another details his difficulties in entering Tibet, the authorities fearing the party to be spies. These letters indicate the hazardous nature of these journeys as well as the excitement of the discoveries. On Kingdon Ward's return, Mr. Grove Annesley received his share of the seed. It was now up to him, as it was to each subscriber, to raise his own seed. Not all succeeded, but failures could be made up by trading successes with other subscribers.

As the rhododendron garden developed, the Dublin drive was closed to wheeled traffic so that it could become the principal walk. It serpentines elegantly through the trees, now amid bold groups of Chinese and Himalayan rhododendrons. *R. decorum, yunnanense,* and *cerasinum,* with flowers of white, blush, and scarlet respectively, are some of those introduced by Kingdon Ward. There are also many colorful *R. cinnabarinum* and *griersonianum.* No rhododendrons have been used more than the Ward introductions for breeding new hybrids, many of which are grown at Annes Grove close to their parents and provide interesting comparisons.

In among the shrubs are some fine trees, including the drooping juniper (*Juniperus recurva*), an immense willow-leaf podocarp (*Podocarpus salignus*), and fine specimens of Wilson and Watson magnolias.

*Annes Grove*

The third of the linked gardens is the water garden on the valley floor. Before Richard Grove Annesley began, there was not even a path down to this area. The river Awbeg, its beauties sung by Edmund Spenser, who began work on *The Faerie Queene* at nearby Kilcolman Castle, flowed quietly at the bottom. Richard Grove Annesley's first step was to divert the river, using a battalion of soldiers from the nearby army barracks at Fermoy, so that it flowed nearer and within view of the house. When doing so, he had a number of weirs and rapids made to break the water's flow. Early on—as is always wise—he planted trees, tall Lawson cypress in variety that make soaring spires against the sky today, and water-loving poplar and willow along the river bank. Their light foliage flickers in summer breezes and the willows' stems glow with warm color in the low winter sunlight. He then planted long reaches of bamboo by the waterside as background and shelter for the smaller plants. (Unfortunately, the bamboo died in the winter of 1981–82, necessitating their removal by the thousand. Their death highlights the problem of maintenance in an historic garden and poses a creative challenge to the present generation.) Huge clumps of gunnera accentuate the bends in the river. Along the banks between, high color is given by long drifts of astilbe, rodgersia, daylilies, and, later, hydrangeas. Bistorts (polygonums) and Australian flax are also seen. One dramatic patch of yellow is composed of an enormous bed of *Primula florindae* growing in mud. This candelabra primula was introduced by Frank Kingdon Ward, who

called it after his wife, Florinda. This uniquely large patch requires considerable maintenance, for the plants must be constantly divided to remain healthy.

The conservation of this extensive garden on many different levels has required careful thought. For example, although many new paths have been opened up, the plantings have been deliberately allowed to grow a little wilder. The garden's essence has been maintained, however, and in many ways the change has resulted in an increased romanticism and a greater contrast with the more meticulously maintained walled and woodland gardens.

William Donnellan, the last of the dedicated gardeners who worked under Richard Grove Annesley's personal direction, has recently retired. Two new gardeners of a much younger generation have started work under the supervision of Jane and Patrick Grove Annesley. Many young rhododendrons propagated from Richard Grove Annesley's original introductions have been extensively planted in the woodland garden, and the Annesleys are now adding Mediterranean plants (for example, clumps of cistus), collected on occasional expeditions to the mountains of Crete, in sunny niches on the limestone cliff above the river.

The garden is now open to the public five days a week during the season. Despite this activity and the building of a new car park (very discreetly placed), Annes Grove remains very much a family garden, retaining that atmosphere of quiet but beautiful seclusion for which, after all, gardens are created.

*In the 1920s, Richard Grove Annesley discovered an unexpected vein of acid soil running through his otherwise limestone land. Here he made a rhododendron garden by clearing the thick woodland to create the light, dappled shade enjoyed by these plants.*

*The Gardens of Ireland*

# Ilnacullin

• • • • • • • • • • • • • • • • •

COUNTY CORK
The National Parks and Monuments Service of the
Office of Public Works

An island is an ideal garden site. Separated from the mainland, it can become a blessed retreat. Exotic architecture and vegetation can convey the impression, however fleetingly, of Eden before the Fall. This sense of a private paradise has led gardeners over many centuries to create gardens on islands.

Ilnacullin, in Irish "the island of holly," is the old name for the island known more recently as Garinish Island. It is set in one of the most beautiful bays in southwest Ireland, Bantry Bay, which is stippled with islands and girded with woods and mountains. John Annan Bryce (1874–1924), a retired East India merchant who was a native of

*The length of mixed borders in the walled garden is broken by clipped cones of golden privet. In June the predominant colors are red, white, and pink. Potentilla astrosanguinea 'Gibson's Scarlet' is interwoven with pink cistus and white iberis.*

*Preceding pages:*
*Purple columbines and yellow-flowering Jerusalem sage line the approach to one of Peto's pedimented gateways.*

*The open colonnade of the Casita surrounds a tea house. The shallow terraces on either side are planted mainly with Australasian leptospermums, olearias, and callistemons, their dull foliage livened in spring with a ribbon of forget-me-not and in summer by haphazard summer bedding.*

Belfast, had been holidaying there for many years before he decided to buy a property in the region. Nothing was available but a goat-ridden reef of about thirty-seven acres in the center of an inlet known as Glengariff Bay. Despite the reservations of his friends, Bryce bought it in 1910 and determined to build a house and garden.

There was, however, no soil to speak of on the island. He was forced to arrange the transport of many boatloads of good soil from the mainland. Even then, rock was so close to the surface that holes had to be blasted in it to provide a sufficiently deep root run for the trees that Bryce immediately saw were necessary as shelter from the gales blowing up the bay from the Atlantic. He planted many hundreds of Scots and Austrian pine, and of two wind-resistant conifers from California— Monterey pine and cypress—without which it would have been impossible to make many of the Irish coastal gardens of the last century. Once they were established in the moist air and temperate climate of the region, their growth was rewarding— one Monterey cypress on Ilnacullin grew fifty feet in twelve years.

Bryce was a knowledgeable plantsman, described once by a neighbor as "a walking encyclopedia" of plants, but he was aware of the need for strong garden design. So he consulted an Englishman, Harold Peto (1854–1933), one of the most eminent architects and garden designers of his time, requesting him to draw up plans for the house and garden. Though others must have had reservations as to

whether Peto's formal Italian style of design would be suitable for a bleak Irish island, Bryce's singular vision in employing him has now been justified. The temples and towers he built have been absorbed by the rapid growth of the trees, which allow the whole island to sit comfortably again in its glorious natural setting of mountain and bay. In a garden that is a balance of architecture and horticulture, the scale of the architecture first overwhelms the plants, but as the latter grow, the balance is restored. So it has been at Ilnacullin.

Peto's conception was of an Italianate house on the hill at the end of the island marked by a Martello Tower, a defensive structure built in 1805 against a threatened Napoleonic invasion. From the base of the hill two long vistas would march across the island, each composed of a complex of different but linked spaces. Bryce began by translating Peto's conception of the garden into reality, delaying the commencement of the house. In the end the house was never built, Bryce being content to inhabit a small cottage on the north shore of the island.

The two vistas are of contrasting character: that on the sheltered landward side of the island is formal, with gardens enclosed by walls and terraces and ornamented with statuary and temples; the vista on the exposed, seaward side is informal, bounded by banks and trees and ornamented with rocks and a natural-looking pool.

The formal gardens begin with a kitchen garden below the rock on which the

Viburnum plicatum 'Mariesii' is well placed on gravel, where the tiered branches of white florets have room to spread without restriction.

Opposite page:
The roofless temple, high above the sea, was designed to hold the statue of a goddess, which would be silhouetted against the mountains and the sea.

house was to be built. Like the other formal gardens, it is not on axis with the site of the house, nor with the other gardens. This is prohibited by the natural lie of the ground, and each space is fitted into the rocky terrain as well as possible. But necessity has been turned to advantage, for the shift in direction of each successive garden or group of gardens provides a vital element of surprise. Nor is the kitchen garden level—it would have required too much rock blasting to achieve this, so it rises and falls with the natural levels, creating a further element of surprise. Despite its elegance, the kitchen garden still serves its nominal purpose; wide herbaceous borders backed by espaliered fruit trees screen blocks of vegetables behind. The main walk leads between matching gates at either end. A cross walk focuses on an ancient Roman sarcophagus. Stone-built towers, one of them elevated to make a bell tower, mark two of the corners of the garden. Through the second gate and thickly planted shrub beds that soften the impact of the change of axis is the heart of the garden of Ilnacullin—the great central lawn that acts as a much-needed interval amid the lush surrounding planting. It becomes a resting place for the eye and a green nucleus for the brighter color of the trees and shrubs around.

The end of the lawn is closed with a colonnaded building in classical style called, in the Italian manner, a *casita*. In the center of the building is a teahouse, on the walls of which Bryce hung his collection of old master drawings. One is reminded of Pliny's description of the pavilions of Roman seaside villas of his time in which people would dine on warm summer evenings, gazing out on the moonlit sea.

The climax of the suite of formal gardens, the sunk garden, is reached through the colonnade. Focusing on a lily tank sunk between shallow grass terraces is another classical building, a pavilion with a central arch framing a view of the sea, the mountains, and the sky. Thus, the axis of the garden is prolonged into the distant landscape. The pavilion is reflected in the lily pool, in a manner reminiscent of another garden of ancient Rome, the Viridarium of Pompeii, which had been excavated shortly before Peto began laying out the garden at Ilnacullin. The stone figures, broken capitals, and cracked vases that came to light in the excavations had originally been arranged around the pool, as if in a museum of sculpture. For a similar effect, Peto and Bryce purchased three boatloads of antiquities to place around the pool at Ilnacullin. Many of them are now gone, since Bryce's son was forced to sell them in the Depression of the thirties, but some remain to give a hint of the former impression. Thus ends the suite of formal gardens.

To one side of the great lawn a path winds away over a ridge and then descends to meet the second of the long vistas—the informal one—by which, it was designed, one could return to the house. The path begins on a high terrace with a roofless temple on a rock close to the waters of the bay, with a view of the mountains beyond. A grass walk lined with cypresses leads down with two changes of direction to what is known as The Happy Valley, closed on either side by high outcrops of rock and thick groves of trees. Rambling roses are trained to grow flat over the rocks and so flower in proliferous sheets. In the bottom of the valley a change in direction is marked by a pool, trapezoidal in shape, its banks broken by natural outcrops of rock and softened with clumps of feathery junipers. A screen of bamboos protects it from the winds that blow off the sea creek below and the walk continues up the hill to the Martello Tower on the highest point of the island. Here there is a fine view from the battlements, and the sound of the wind in the trees and the waves on the shore reinforces the impression, already strong, of an enchanted isle.

*The Gardens of Ireland*

*Ilnacullin*

*The sunk garden and lily tank.*

*The arching canes of the bamboo* Arundinaria japonica *lean picturesquely over a lily pond in the Happy Valley. The growth of the water lilies is strictly controlled to allow reflections on the water surface between them.*

This pair of vistas was Peto's contribution to Ilnacullin; Bryce's was in the planting. He quickly realized the climatic advantages of the place in terms of growing a rich collection of trees and shrubs. In particular, he realized the potential of plants from the same latitude in the southern hemisphere as Ilnacullin's in the northern—around 50°. His perception has been fully justified by time. Leptospermums, callistemons, grevilleas, olearias, and acacias from Australia, hoherias and corokias from New Zealand, drimys and ozothamnus from Tasmania flourish, flower, and seed themselves as well as they do in their respective native lands. Plants like embothriums, myrtles, eucryphias, and escallonias from Chile and Argentina, on the other side of the globe but on a similar latitude, also thrive. It is rare for South African species to survive in northern Europe, but on this blessed isle *Virgilia capensis* and *Phygelius capensis*, both—as their names imply—from the Cape, and *Bowkeria gerrardiana*, from Natal, flower and fruit. Peto's buildings and walls support a fascinating collection of climbing plants—for example, no fewer than six species of *Schisandra*, a twining climber with scarlet berries from China, as well as its close relation *Pileostegia viburnoides*. Room has also been found for rhododendrons in that combination of large-leaved forms and tender species that is characteristic of the Irish coastal garden. In between are found interesting perennials such as the Chatham Island forget-me-not and the blue Tibetan poppy.

But Bryce's most lasting contribution was his planting of a collection of tender conifers from the southern hemisphere. Many of them are slow growing and give no promise of developing into more than small trees. Nonetheless they are decorative. *Athrotaxius laxifolia,* one of only three species native to the mountains of Tasmania; *Fitzroya cupressoides,* a species native to the border of Chile and Argentina; *Phyllocladus glaucus* from the north island of New Zealand (the one at Ilnacullin is the only one recorded in the open in either Britain or Ireland); and *Dacrydium cupressinum,* also from New Zealand and at thirty feet the highest recorded in cultivation in these islands, are all exciting. There are, in addition, some rare conifers from the Far East such as *Taiwania cryptomerioides* from the island of Formosa and the very rare *Fokienia hodginsii,* native to China. Bryce added a collection of bonsai from Japan, which was also the source of inspiration for another of his plantings—a group of azaleas clipped into domes on the bank of the central lawn.

Ilnacullin is a rich blend of architecture inspired by many periods and styles and constructed of many different materials, together with plants derived from many corners of the globe. Too indigestible for some, for others a gargantuan feast, no one can deny the sumptuousness of its conception or its impact on an already dramatic natural setting.

*An island makes a perfect site for a garden. Water separates this ideal world of architecture and exotic vegetation from the world outside.*

*The Gardens of Ireland*

# Garinish Island

· · · · · · · · · · · · · · · · · ·

## COUNTY KERRY
### Mr. Cavan G. Browne and Mr. R. Seamus Browne

Ireland's rugged Atlantic coastline is punctuated by deep inlets and harbors. Along their sheltered inner shores many fascinating gardens have been made: Glanleam, Kells Bay, Reen-na-farraha, Ardnagashel, Creagh, Lisselane, Derreen, Rossdohan, and Ilnacullin. Nearby, but farther inland, are the gardens of Dunloe Castle and Muckross House. Some are excellently maintained; others are, at present, somewhat in decline. Perhaps the most fascinating of the Atlantic group are those on islands. Being totally surrounded by water, their microclimate is comparatively mild. Besides, there is something especially magical about making a garden on an island.

In June, the woods are stained mauve by the flowers of Rhododendron ponticum. A native of Eastern Europe, it has naturalized itself in many parts of Ireland, becoming a nuisance, destroying the native vegetation and, in Kerry, the feeding grounds of the native red deer.

Preceding pages:
The geological structure has been exploited in the garden's design. Here a limestone outcrop with a fringe of hosta is enveloped in Rhododendron ponticum and a young tree fern, Dicksonia antarctica, while a many-branched Cordyline australis makes a focal point against the sky.

The house, perched on a plateau of rock, has one of the finest views in Ireland.

Garinish Island was bought by the third earl of Dunraven in about 1860. A well-known scholar and antiquary, he wished to make it a base for his archaeological expeditions in the area, so he commissioned the leading Irish architect James Franklin Fuller to build a house for him. The house is low-slung, perched on a plateau of rock, its eaves reaching almost to the ground in the manner of an Alpine lodge. On the seaward end of the island, only low heathers and furze, sea grasses and pinks provide shelter for the gulls' eggs. The view, however, of the estuary and sea, framed by the misty mountains of the Kenmare and Beara peninsulas, is one of the finest in Ireland. On the landward side there are sheltering groves of native oak, an ideal location in which to garden. However, the earl was not a gardener.

It was his son, the fourth earl, who created the garden. He began, as all good gardeners should, by planting trees to augment the existing groves. He chose Monterey pine (*Pinus radiata*) from California and the Balkan *Rhododendron ponticum*. It is a source of constant surprise that these introduced plants outdo the native ones in withstanding the sea winds.

In laying out the garden, Lord Dunraven cleverly exploited the geological structure of the island. This consists of a series of alternating limestone ridges and gorges crossing the island from east to west. The ridges were seized upon as opportunities for making natural rock gardens, the shallow gorges as locations for developing wild woodland and shrub gardens. So it is a garden of constant surprise. Nothing compares with the excitement of climbing up the paths to one of the ridges only to discover yet another glade of subtropical plants, and, in other spots, to discover

oneself by the seashore, or on a plateau with a view of mountain or sea.

It is often remarked that gardeners in the southwest corner of Ireland are fortunate in having exceptionally mild winters and moist summers, ensuring an abundant growth of plants. But the southwest also has disadvantages—thin soil and high winds—that often have to be overcome by elaborate preparations. Before the shallow gorges at Garinish could be gardened, for example, it was necessary to fill them to a depth of many feet with soil from the mainland, to provide level or softly undulating lawns and a deep root run for trees and shrubs. Many hundreds of yards of drains had to be laid under the lawns to take off the rainwater that runs off the ridges into the gorges. Before the rock gardens could be made, steps had to be cut into the limestone to give access, vegetation cleared to expose the often beautiful face of the rock, and pockets and clefts in the stone filled with soil for planting. This is not a onetime job, however. Drains must be constantly unblocked, the abundant natural growth contained and directed, and the soil pockets replenished. These are the special concerns of Seamus Browne and his wife, Bernadette, who garden Garinish today, as they were of the gardeners of the past.

When ready for planting, each glen or gorge was given a distinct theme. One became a water garden, its pool fed by the underground drainage system. Thick drifts of Asiatic primulas now decorate its margins. Another glen was planted with cordyline palms and eucalyptus. About this time, toward the end of the nineteenth century, it was becoming generally known that plants from the Australasian continent were particularly suited to the Irish climate. Lord Dunraven took full advan-

*In one of the sheltered glens that cross Garinish Island is an avenue of the Australian tree fern*, Dicksonia antarctica.

*The view from the house, over the wild garden to the shoreline with its sheltering groves of native oak,* Quercus petraea, *and Scots pine,* Pinus sylvestris. *In the background are the mainland and the Derrynasaggart Mountains.*

tage of the experiments in the acclimatization of these plants his gardening neighbors, Lord Lansdowne at Derreen and Surgeon-Major Heard at Rossdohan, were carrying out. He also had the benefit of advice from his brother-in-law, Lord Barrymore, who was at that time developing the magnificent arboretum at Fota, County Cork. As in all gardening circles, there was a free exchange of plants. Although each glen had a specific planting theme, it was not adhered to rigidly, as it might have been in a purely botanical collection, and Lord Dunraven added plants to provide variety and contrast. Thus he followed the recommendations of William Robinson in *The Wild Garden.* For example, in the glen of the eucalyptus, he planted what is now a splendid specimen of *Daphniphyllum macropodum.* Its glistening, apple-green leaves bring the silvery gray coloring of the eucalyptus sharply into focus.

Another valley was planted with magnolias and camellias, among them a *Magnolia x wiesneri,* its large flowers exuding a powerful scent of pineapple. Yet another glen was planted with tree ferns, *Dicksonia antarctica,* their number being considerably augmented by examples removed from neighboring Rossdohan following Surgeon-Major Heard's death in 1923. Near these grows a camphor tree (*Cinnamonum camphora*), a tree of economic importance as the source of camphor and one of only two in Irish gardens known to the author.

By 1913, the collection of plants had grown to the point where Lord Dunraven had a catalogue printed, a copy of which can still be seen in the house. From it we can see how widely he ranged in his search for plants. He combed nurseries in the

*The Gardens of Ireland*

mild climates of Cornwall, the Scilly and Channel Isles, as well as those long-gone but still renowned Northern Ireland nurseries, Smith of Newry and Davis of Hillsborough. On one occasion he imported a consignment of hydrangeas from Japan.

After Lord Dunraven's death in 1926, there was a hiatus in garden development until the island was bought by Mr. Reginald Browne about thirty years ago. His wife did much to restore many years of neglect, replenishing the plantings, particularly of camellias and magnolias in the glens, and of cistus, helianthemums, and lithospermums on the rocks. Rare saxifrages now mix with the sheets of pink oxalis on the rock shelves, and curtains of the Crimson Glory Vine (*Vitis coignetiae*) hang down over the heather-clad faces.

The island is now owned by their sons, Cavan and Seamus Browne, and a new phase of the garden has begun. Seamus Browne in particular has taken great interest in it. He has planted many new camellias, magnolias, rhododendrons, and acacias, many obtained from that reservoir of good plants, the South Down nurseries in Cornwall. The acquisition of new plants is not easy, as Mr. Browne has insisted on maintaining the high standard and rarity of the plants in the garden. Very often they can be obtained only, and with difficulty, from abroad. His difficulty may, however, turn out to the advantage of others who garden in the mild climate of counties Cork and Kerry, because he hopes to propagate these plants and offer them for sale through a nursery he plans to set up. Thus Garinish should continue to influence gardening in this southwest corner of Ireland in the future as it has in the past.

*The Gardens of Ireland*

# Derreen

• • • • • • • • • • • • • • • • • • •

COUNTY KERRY
The Honorable David Bigham

Kenmare Bay is a turbulent estuary running inland from the sea between high mountain ranges on the southwest coast of Ireland. Although
it is a funnel for Atlantic gales, there are some sheltered inlets. In one
of these, in a superbly beautiful setting, is the ninety-acre peninsula on
which the house and garden of Derreen stand.

The estate of Derreen has descended in the family of the present
owner from the seventeenth century, but it was not until the nineteenth
century that the afforestation of the surrounding mountains and the
development of the gardens began. The third marquess of Lansdowne
began by planting oak, ash, sycamore, and beech, as well as Scots and

The complex tracery of old trees throws a
dappled light on mixed plantings of tree
rhododendrons, dwarf Japanese azaleas, and
a meadow of bluebells.

Preceding pages:
Tree ferns, Dicksonia antarctica, spread
themselves by self-sown sporelings,
particularly in damp drainage channels,
blocking them and so causing a constant need
for maintenance.

A large, dome-shaped outcrop of rock emerges
from the lawn in front of the house.

maritime pine, but it was his grandson, the fifth marquess, who carried out the
extensive planting program that transformed the bare rock and scrub oak of the
property into the luxuriant woodland we see today. By 1884 four hundred acres
were planted, largely with the newly introduced giant conifers of northwest America, some of which, notably giant arborvitae, *Thuja plicata*, and western hemlock,
*Tsuga heterophylla*, are over 140 feet tall today. He also realized the potential of
the soft climate of Kerry, which has seventy or eighty inches of rain a year and
rare frosts, for growing the exotic plants then being introduced from all over the
temperate world. For over fifty years, from 1870 until the 1920s (except for the
period between 1883 and 1894, when he was governor general of Canada and then
viceroy of India), Lord Lansdowne spent three months of the year at Derreen,
forming and then improving one of the finest subtropical gardens in Britain or
Ireland.

He began by enlarging the house to the designs of the Irish architect James
Franklin Fuller, and clearing the wood and scrub around it to make an open,
gently undulating lawn dotted with pine. Leading out from it he cleared a series of
long grassy rides, which eventually give on to the seashore. Around the fringes of
the lawn and along the sides of the rides, with dense woodland for a background,
he began to plant wide, serpentine borders of the trees and shrubs for which
Derreen is noted. Now tall trees lift one's eye to the mountains behind. A huge

*The Gardens of Ireland*

*The Chilean fire bush*, Embothrium coccineum, *bears its profusion of orange-scarlet flowers in May and June.*

*A zigzag timber footbridge leads to an islet thickly clothed with* Phormium tenax, Rhododendron ponticum, *and native gorse under a canopy of Scots pine.*

Monterey cypress, *Cupressus macrocarpa*, was planted by Lord Lansdowne's father in 1856. Eucalyptuses, in particular the Tasmanian blue gum, *Eucalyptus globulus*, which Lord Lansdowne planted in 1870, are now among the tallest in cultivation. A Japanese cedar, *Cryptomeria japonica*, planted ten years later leans over the rock garden walk at an angle of forty-five degrees, yet is still among the largest in these islands. It is sixty feet high and one of its four arms has a ten-foot girth.

In front of his planting of conifers from the American northwest, now very large trees, Lord Lansdowne—a true gardener of his generation—planted over one hundred tree rhododendron hybrids. These were obtained from the great English breeders like the nursery firm of Waterer, which named one of their new hybrids 'Lady Lansdowne' after his wife. Before long, all but a handful had to be cut down —they grew into vast trees, crowding each other and excluding all light. Later he forsook hybrid for species rhododendrons collected in the wild in India, China, and Tibet. It was when he was viceroy of India that he began to collect the Himalayan rhododendrons that are now such a feature of the garden. From the expeditions of the great plant hunter E. H. "Chinese" Wilson he received seed from the English nursery firm of Veitch for whom Wilson collected. From Sir Frederick Moore of the Botanic Gardens in Dublin, he also received Wilson rhododendrons. Later he subscribed to the plant-hunting expeditions of Kingdon Ward to the

Sunlight illuminates the elegant architecture
of the moisture-loving Gunnera manicata.


Opposite page:
On a natural carpet of bluebells and long
grass, the domes of old Rhododendron
arboreum hybrids reflect light up into the
sombre shadows of the spirelike conifers
Thuja plicata.

Rhododendron x loderi 'King George' is
remarkable for its large, fragrant flowers,
pink-tinted in the bud.

Eastern Himalayas and to that of Cox on the Burma-Yunnan border, receiving his
share of the seed collected. Now *Rhododendron sinogrande*, *R. delavayi*, *R. falconeri*, and *R. niveum* from Bhutan, Sikkim, and Tibet are tall in the borders
along the edge of the glades. Though the rhododendrons finish flowering by the
end of the spring, summer-flowering trees and shrubs like New Zealand hoherias,
myrtles, hydrangeas, and buddleias are generously intermixed with them. Also, at
frequent intervals are rich plantings of Australian flax, cordyline palms (dracaenas), and bamboos, their architectural foliage providing unchanging focal
points throughout the year. So, though Derreen is of great interest as a rhododendron garden, fine evergreen trees and shrubs, and many summer-flowering ones,
make it enthralling in every season.

Tucked away in sheltered backwaters, out of reach of the winds that blow up
the rides from the sea, are the wattles of New Zealand and Chilean crinodendrons.
Most spectacular of all are groves of the tall tree fern, *Dicksonia antarctica*, the
tallest of which were planted around 1900. The oldest specimens have put on little
growth over the last twenty-five years and now have less luxuriant fronds than their
younger progeny. Along the walk known as the King's Oozy, in the shade of giant
blue gum and bamboo, they constantly reproduce themselves with hundreds of
self-sown spores emerging from the ground underneath and, particularly, from the
drainage channels. The complex architecture of the great fronds of these giant
primitive plants, once said to have covered the globe, shed a kaleidoscope of light

and shade on the long grass below. When the wind rises off the bay, these fronds and branches begin to oscillate in compound rhythms against the sky. Walking through them, it is easy to imagine oneself in some remote and untamed jungle.

In the early 1950s, Derreen was inherited by Lord Lansdowne's granddaughter, Viscountess Mersey, a keen gardener, who restored and extended the plantings, adding tender rhododendrons of the *maddenii* and *edgeworthii* series and tender Mexican pines such as *Pinus montezumae* and *Pinus patula*. Her plantings of large-leaved *Rhododendron macabeanum* are splendidly at home and in scale with the curling contours of the mountains.

Derreen is now owned by her son, the Honorable David Bigham, who opens it to the public during the summer. In a garden in a climate like this he faces the problem of restraining rather than promoting the growth of many plants. Throughout the garden a rich patina of moss, lichens, ferns, and saxifrages covers rocks, paths, and tree trunks. Gaultherias and pernettyas threaten to engulf the paths. Tree ferns seed in the drainage channels and block them. Colonies of *Rhododendron ponticum*, myrtles, and arbutus may overwhelm weaker yet prized specimens of other plants. The key to the garden's maintenance is watchfulness and constant choice between one plant and another to ensure that the balance between exotic and wilding, between the strong and the weak, between open and planted space, between garden and mountain background, is held for future generations. It is a task that is being performed admirably under Mr. Bigham's direction.

The Gardens of Ireland

# Mount Congreve

• • • • • • • • • • • • • • • •

COUNTY WATERFORD
Mr. and Mrs. Ambrose Congreve

The great white house of Mount Congreve has been the home of the Congreve family since 1725. Among famous members of the family have been William Congreve, the Restoration dramatist, and another William who, it is claimed, invented matches and the first military rocket. The present head of the family, Ambrose Congreve, is widely known for the extraordinary garden he has made in the last thirty years.

Before the last war, one of Mr. Congreve's aunts, Lady Bessborough, was a great friend of Lionel de Rothschild, whose garden at Exbury in Hampshire, England, was, and still is, one of the great rhododendron

*A late-summer combination of pink* Anemone japonica, *fuchsia, and* Hypericum elatum, *with bright red fruits, flanks the entrance to the walled garden.*

*Preceding pages:*
*In 1955, Mr. Congreve began in earnest to make clearings in the woodland, creating pools of dappled light in which flowering trees and shrubs might flourish. The rhododendron beds, often dozens of yards wide, are frequently edged with Exbury and other hybrid azaleas.*

*The great house, like many Irish houses, is on a Palladian plan of a center block and a pair of service wings. It has been in the Congreve family since 1725. The approach gives no hint of the color-filled gardens beyond.*

*Opposite page:*
*Banks of hydrangeas, hundreds of yards long, extend along the river walks.*

gardens of the world. Indeed, Mr. de Rothschild named one of his great rhododendron hybrids 'Lady Bessborough' for her, and it is now seen in gardens everywhere. As a young man, Mr. Congreve frequently visited Exbury and it was there that he conceived the idea of making a great garden in Ireland.

The sites of Exbury and Mount Congreve are very similar. They both consist of thickly wooded hills sloping towards a river. Great rhododendron hybrids like those that have made Exbury famous have not yet emerged from the garden of Mount Congreve but it has excelled its model in other ways. While at Exbury there are only two trees of *Magnolia campbellii*, the giant pink tulip tree of the Himalayas, at Mount Congreve there are more than eighty in one of the riverside walks alone. Already of great beauty, in years to come these will provide a spring spectacle of unrivaled splendor.

It comes as a surprise to visitors that many Irish gardens are hidden from the view of the houses to which they belong and such is the garden at Mount Congreve. Driving up to the house, one is given no hint of its color-filled gardens lying deep in the surrounding woods. The setting seems to be a piece of traditional old parkland graced with many mature hardwood trees. Mr. Congreve has added groups of purple-leaved trees such as the Norway maple known as 'Faassen's Black', which enjoys the darkest of all purple leaves. As a low fringe at the base of the wings of the house, he has planted hybrids of Australian flax in variegated yellows and purples. These muted colors soften the severely classical lines of the house.

Even walking through the house onto the north side, you have no immediate clue. At first you see a simple grass terrace enclosed by yew hedges—a sober setting underlining the architectural restraint of the house. Then you realize that this is but a green platform from which to view the theater of woodland beyond lit up in season by the flowering of thousands of magnolias and rhododendrons. The sobriety of mood is broken only by some wheelbarrow seats, a pair of imposing gates, long hydrangea borders, and in the middle of the lawn a fountain decorated with a statue of a boy with a swan.

It is only when you leave this space through one of a pair of gilded wrought-iron gates and descend via sets of steps into the trees that the garden gradually unfolds. As the eye adjusts to the dappled shade, great swathes of flower color, often hundreds of yards long, begin to register. "Woodland gardens should not have all their secrets exposed from one or two vantage points," Mr. Congreve stresses when explaining his approach to garden design. Paths lead off through the trees over the undulating ground and the secrets of the gardens of Mount Congreve are revealed.

Mr. Congreve places emphasis on making each group of plants as large as possible: "Plants should not be scattered about the garden and repetitions of the same mixtures should be avoided. In any planting, the question of scale ought to be considered, and little groups of color dotted about in an extensive shrubbery or herbaceous border do not, in my opinion, look well. Therefore, if you plant three *Rhododendron thomsonii* or twenty, plant them together in a group to make a bold color effect." So, in 1955, when Mr. Congreve began in earnest to make clearings in his woodland, creating pools of light in which groups of flowering trees and shrubs might flourish, he planted in groups of not less than six of each type and often in greater numbers. The results of this bold policy are now evident at every hand. Banks of hydrangeas, sometimes hundreds of yards in length, extend along the lowest series of walks, close to the river. There are more than five hundred camellia cultivars. Giant-leaved Himalayan rhododendrons, planted in large groups, will, when mature, provide dramatic reflections of the flower color of their

*The Gardens of Ireland*

*A rock garden has been carved out of an old quarry face recently. An artificial waterfall, its descent carefully regulated by both natural and artificially made fissures, has been designed to cascade into the pool below.*

native mountainsides. For example, there is one group of no less than fifty *Rhododendron macabeanum*, which open their large trusses of yellow flowers in March or April. There are many large groups of *Rhododendron sinogrande*, with flowers in huge creamy-white trusses. The rhododendron beds, often twenty yards wide, are fronted by wide borders of smaller Exbury and other hybrid and species azaleas, or dwarf purple Japanese maples or potentillas. Some are edged with lines of boulders, where in season sheets of campanula and saxifrage flower in the joints. Planting these plots was a major undertaking, but maintaining them is an even greater task, as they must be constantly sprayed against rhododendron fly, bud blast, and petal wilt.

South American fire bushes (*Embothrium coccineum*), their flowers like scarlet sparks, have established large young colonies of their seedlings around them. The allied telopeas from Tasmania, with their less strident color, flower later. Large masses of *Cotoneaster* 'Rothschildianus' (bred at Exbury) and *C.* 'Santa Monica' berry the woods below the house terrace in winter with yellow and red respectively. In another section of the garden floribunda roses are planted in a manner usually reserved for rhododendrons—in large informal patches of a single variety. A long walk descending the hill to the river has deep borders of mixed rugosa roses, backed by *Magnolia x soulangiana* hybrids, on either hand. Spring bulbs are massed in their thousands and even the trees are gardened—spring-flowering clematis, climbing honeysuckle and roses, and, most dramatic of all, the actinidia with the triple-colored leaf, *Actinidia kolomikta*, are being planted to scale the trunks of lofty oak and beech.

Throughout the garden, the froth of leaf and flower is stabilized by the solid spires of upright conifers planted in groups of three, five, or more. The incense cedar (*Libocedrus decurrens*), Brewer's spruce (*Picea breweriana*), weeping Nootka cypress (*Chamaecyparis nootkatensis* 'Pendula'), the Japanese umbrella pine (*Schiadopitys verticillata*), Wisselii Lawson cypress (*Chamaecyparis lawsoniana* 'Wisselii'), the smooth Arizona cypress (*Cupressus glabra*), and the blue wellingtonia (*Sequoiadendron giganteum glauca*) are among the conifers used for this purpose. Where two or more paths cross, focal plantings have been made. *Magnolia x wiesneri* presides over one crossing so that it wafts its pineapple scent over each of the walks. Bold clumps of the Mexican *Beschorneria yuccoides*, which in flower look like gigantic lobsters, preside over another.

Frequently, some rare tree catches the eye of the dendrologist. *Neolitsea sericea*, an aromatic evergreen from tropical Asia, and *Meliosma oldhamii* from Korea are two. But there are also collections of unusual trees like those of the genus *Azara*, with scented yellow flowers, and *Phyllocladus*, the curious Australian genus of trees and shrubs whose branchlets are flattened out to resemble and perform the functions of leaves. Eucalyptus are not represented, as Mr. Congreve dislikes them.

Perhaps the most spectacular period of the year in the garden is when the magnolias flower. Hundreds of Asiatic species and their hybrids light up the glades in March and April. The flowers of *Magnolia campbellii, campbellii mollicomata, x veitchii,* and *heptapeta* open first, to be followed by those of *M. sprengeri* 'Diva' and *salicifolia*. Next come many *M. x soulangiana* hybrids, *M. x loebneri,* and *M. hypoleuca*. Finally in June, the display ends with the last flowers of *Magnolia quinquepeta* and its hybrids. Recently, a so-far unique magnolia was discovered on a visit to the garden by Sir Peter Smithers, the magnolia specialist. Its flowers

often have twenty-four or more individual petals, and he has named it, provisionally, *Magnolia multipetala*.

In contrast to this overwhelming botanic and horticultural richness, there are many areas of open, sunlit lawn. Thus the pace of the garden is varied. Mr. Congreve explains: "Grass should be used in both formal and informal gardens. Formal lawns, as well as informal ones, with grass paths winding out of sight, can do much to highlight tree and shrub plantings, cooling down the mass of colors."

Each of the lawns at Mount Congreve has a different theme. One is fringed with floribunda roses, another is punctuated by a noble sweet chestnut, yet another is darkened with dwarf purple Japanese maples. On occasion a seat marks a spot where the woods open to reveal a view of the surrounding countryside. Further variation is provided by a series of dramatic architectural incidents, sometimes of breathtaking scale. In an old quarry, an artificial waterfall tumbles in many streams, following fissures carefully dynamited and cut out of the stone, down a cliff face into a pool below. At another point, a high, southwest-facing wall designed to protect tender plants is pierced by an opening in the shape of a Chinese moon gate. It frames a balustrade in Chinese style, and below is a Chinese pagoda, recently built and painted in vivid Chinese red, yellow, and green. The pagoda, too, occupies a space once quarried, then dynamited and planted with alpines by gardeners who were lowered down the quarry face on ropes. (It is still tended in

*The Georgian greenhouse, recently restored, is a background for a hot color scheme of red dahlias, orange red-hot pokers, and pink phlox, all grown and maintained to standards unequalled in Ireland.*

*A sculpture of a Commedia dell'Arte figure decorates the walled garden.*

the same way.) Beyond is a panorama of the broad river Suir, tidal at this point, and to the north, the rolling hills of neighboring County Kilkenny.

The show in many of the great rhododendron gardens of the world is over with the end of spring. Not so at Mount Congreve, for herbaceous borders, planted and maintained to flower-show standards, come into their own after the flowering of the rhododendrons.

Mount Congreve's walled garden is reached through a gateway that opens to reveal a pair of sloping lawns, each flanked with herbaceous borders. Designed to be at their peak in August, their vivid oranges and reds, mauves and purples, lemon yellows and silvers vie for attention. An ancient maidenhair tree (*Ginkgo biloba*), of a very unusual domical form, presides over the upper lawn. The Georgian greenhouse has small panes of glass indicating its construction in the period before plate glass was manufactured. Under its sheltering roof are rows and rows of potted lilies, fuchsias, amaryllis, and nerines, which are carried up to the house to decorate its rooms. On the lower lawn is an octagonal lily pool with, nearby, one of the many gaily painted wheelbarrow seats that are placed throughout the garden. Their curious design dates from the eighteenth century and was devised so that the seat could be wheeled around to take the best advantage of sun or shade. Light relief is supplied by a painted figure of the Turk from the *Commedia dell'Arte*.

Through another gate, a second walled garden comes as a surprise. It is sharply angular in shape and is almost entirely filled by a large sheet of water. The plants in its margins were chosen primarily for their foliage effect rather than for their flower color, which makes this garden a dramatic contrast with the first. A collection of over a hundred different forms of Japanese iris has been given to Mr. Congreve by Sir Peter Smithers from his remarkable garden on Lake Lugano. Their swordlike leaves contrast with the flat pads of the lilies floating on the water. The clustered spikes of a Chusan palm break the skyline. The lush fronds of gunnera and the plumes of bamboo wave gently in the breezes. We are reminded that it was an Irishman, William Robinson, who pioneered the natural garden style and wrote of the beauty of form and foliage in a garden as opposed to that of flower color.

Yet a third walled garden lies beyond. It is mainly devoted to the very practical function of a plant-propagating unit in which young camellias and azaleas are raised for export abroad. In the current manner, it was established to help defray some of the expenses of the garden, which now extends over one hundred acres. Down the center of this garden, Mr. Congreve has laid out borders to fill the so-called June gap in flowering. One pair has ranks of peonies and delphiniums, the other is devoted to early-flowering herbaceous plants. In one corner are frames in which grow rows of young rhododendron seedlings bred by Mr. Congreve. His breeding program is designed to develop late-flowering rhododendrons in colors other than white, which hitherto is all that has been available. If he succeeds, he will have added a very valuable range of plants to our gardens.

A garden of this magnitude—maintained at this level of perfection—is hard to assimilate and describe. It is difficult to believe that it has been the work of one man—with the assistance of a gardening staff, of course. At present the staff numbers thirty-five, divided between the garden and the nursery, under the direction of the head gardener, Mr. Dool. And there is still much to be done. Mr. Congreve is actively developing new areas and planting them. Summer-flowering clematis, in dozens of different varieties, are being trained to grow up an assembly of timber tripods over ten feet high. A new rock garden has been made on a sunny upper plateau. The huge task of thinning the plantations awaits him. Thousands of plants,

having grown up so quickly that they begin to crowd one another, will have to be transplanted in order to give the remaining ones space in which to mature. Mr. Congreve has, however, planned carefully for the future, as the garden will eventually be transferred to the ownership of the state.

What relevance has such a large garden for the average garden owner of today? First, plants from all over the world are being tested here. The results of these tests can be applied in a garden of any size. Secondly, the garden's fine foliage and floral effects can be copied on a smaller scale. This garden also has a function in teaching those who are responsible for planting our public parks, roadsides, and institutions ways of using flowering trees and shrubs on a large scale. Above all, a garden such as this can be appreciated for itself, as the consummate work of art it is.

*A monumental tree of heaven, Ginkgo biloba, with an uncharacteristic domed head, forms the focus of the walled garden. Here its complex shadows fall on a pattern of stone sets, and on blue and white bluebells.*

*The Gardens of Ireland*

# Malahide Castle

• • • • • • • • • • • • • • • • • • •

COUNTY DUBLIN
Dublin County Council

Gardens are as varied in character as their creators. Some rely mainly on design, some on architecture, still others may be botanical or collector's gardens. The garden at Malahide is preeminently a collector's garden reflecting the erudition and passion of its creator, one of the finest plantsmen of our time.

The present castle of Malahide, situated on the coast about nine miles north of Dublin, is about five hundred years old, though the estate, until its sale in 1976, had been in the possession of the Talbot family for nearly eight hundred years. The castle is an amalgam of constructions of different periods united into one picturesque whole. It contains

*From the castle roof, the shrubbery linking it to the walled garden can be seen. The grassy foliage of pampas grass, Australian flax, and blue sheep's fescue contrasts with the solid form of an upright Irish juniper.*

*Preceding pages:*
*The castle door is festooned in yellow-flowering* Dendromecon rigida *and* Fremontodendron *'California Glory'. Their yellow is reflected in lime-green* Euphorbia wulfenii *and, at left, bright yellow Jerusalem sage.*

*The castle, which dates from the fifteenth century, is framed in park trees.*

some splendid apartments still furnished with the ancestral portraits and furniture of the Talbots, though much was dispersed in the sale of ten years ago. Set in a park of 250 acres, the castle lacked a garden of any consequence until Milo, the seventh Lord Talbot de Malahide, began to make one in the 1950s. By the time of his death in 1973, it had become one of the finest private botanical gardens in the world. In 1976, the castle and its park and gardens were sold to Dublin County Council, which opened part of them to the public as the Talbot Botanic Gardens.

The garden, covering an area of about twenty acres around the castle, contains a collection of over five thousand different plant species and cultivars. As the soil was alkaline, Lord Talbot was unable to grow rhododendrons and camellias, the great glories of so many Irish gardens. He was further restricted by the fact that this is the driest part of Ireland and is subject to frequent severe frosts and desiccating winds, which blow across the flat countryside from the Irish Sea. To combat these he cleared or thinned many old trees around the castle and planted new sheltering hedges—*Escallonia rubra macrantha*, *Cotoneaster conspicuus*, *Olearia macrodonta* 'Major', and *Griselinia littoralis*—which enclose large, informal lawns on all sides. Within this newly established shelter he began to plant his collections.

His collecting was at first influenced by the fact that he had also inherited an estate on the Australian island of Tasmania. He began to experiment with the

*The Gardens of Ireland*

introduction of Tasmanian plants to his Irish garden, specializing in olearias, of which he had probably the world's finest collection in cultivation. These big evergreen shrubs with asterlike flowers are not so conspicuous as many other flowering shrubs, but being resistant to salt winds, they are particularly useful for maritime gardens like that at Malahide. Lord Talbot's interest in olearias has resulted in the naming of one hybrid *Olearia* 'Talbot de Malahide' in his honor. His collecting of ozothamnus, another Australasian family of flowering shrubs, was particularly fortunate, for when a bush fire in 1964 extinguished all apparent traces of *Ozothamnus antennaria* in its wild habitat in Tasmania, Lord Talbot was able to give plants, which he had raised from seed collected many years before, to restock the area. This is yet another example of the important part gardens play in the conservation of the wild plants of the world. Because the climate did not permit a complete collection of Tasmanian plants in his Irish garden, Lord Talbot collected them in book form instead, by financing the publication of *The Endemic Flora of Tasmania*, written by Dr. Winifred M. Curtis and beautifully illustrated by Margaret Stones, in six volumes.

Lord Talbot's collections were not, however, exclusively confined to Australasian plants. He was a diplomat who travelled extensively, and after his retirement, he continued to travel to collect wild seed for his garden. Between 1961 and 1968 he made journeys for this purpose to Ethiopia, Chile, Kashmir, Mexico, Afghani-

*A line of Chusan palms,* Trachycarpus fortunei, *hides the nursery beds on the left, while the long border on the right contains collections of ceanothus, olearia, and leptospermum. In the right foreground is the Tasmanian endemic,* Ozothamnus ledifolius.

*A collector is fascinated by the unique and the curious. Here is a rare form, with serrated petals, of the common* Clematis montana.

*Opposite page:*
Fremontodendron *'California Glory', a free-flowering hybrid of* Fremontodendron mexicanum *and* F. californicum *raised at the Rancho Santa Ana Botanic Garden at Orange County, California.*

*Overleaf:*
*The tabulated architecture of the branches of an old cedar of Lebanon is seen to advantage from the castle roof.*

stan, and Nepal. Nevertheless, he did not overlook local opportunities for adding to his collections: his garden notebook for 1971 records his finding a form of ribbongrass, *Phalaris arundinacea*, on Malahide Railway Station.

His passion for growing tender plants resulted in the erection of special structures to protect them. A high wall, known as the Tresco Wall, was built to shelter a collection of plants given to him by Lieutenant Commander T. A. Dorrien Smith, whose garden at Tresco Abbey in the Scilly Isles off the southwest coast of England has a climate mild enough to grow one of the most remarkable collections of southern hemisphere plants in Europe. Among the exotic plants from Tresco now growing on the wall are *Bomarea kalbreyeri*, a climbing amaryllid from Colombia in tropical South America, *Hypericum ruwenzoriense* from the legendary Mountains of the Moon in Central Africa, and *Senecio leucostachys* (or *vira-vira*) from Patagonia in southern Argentina.

In his later years Lord Talbot acquired plants not so much from his own expeditions as from those of others and through seed exchanges with botanic gardens and institutions all over the world. To shelter many of these treasures too tender to grow in the open he built a number of greenhouses, including an alpine house and a temperate house known as the Cambridge House.

Although Malahide is primarily a collector's garden, in which design and pictorial interest are of secondary importance, there are moments of elegance and picturesque beauty within it. The castle itself makes a handsome background for a range of climbing plants. The front door is festooned with two yellow-flowered shrubs from California, *Dendromecon rigida* and a *Fremontodendron* hybrid. Reaching a height of thirty feet, they clamber around the mullioned window of the Oak Room above. Associated with them on the entrance front are *Sophora tetraptera* and a double Banksian rose, both also yellow-flowered, together with the pale white *Jasminum polyanthum* and brilliant blue *Ceanothus griseus horizontalis*. Yellows, whites, blues, and pale pinks are the predominating colors at Malahide. They make for quite a different color key from the scarlets and oranges more usually seen in Irish gardens.

To the east, the castle walls, with the tall windows of the mediaeval Great Hall, the ruined fifteenth-century church nearby, and the buttressed garden wall provide romantic settings for the sometimes strangely assorted plants of a collector. Growing here are *Magnolia delavayi, Rosa chinensis* 'Old Blush', a large paulownia which rises from a mounded heather garden, and one of the most beautiful of coniferous trees, *Cupressus lusitanica* 'Glauca Pendula', which was grown from a cutting taken in the garden of Rowallane in Northern Ireland. The windows of the two Georgian drawing rooms look out onto the huge durmast oak, with a spread of forty-two yards, and the giant cedar of Lebanon underplanted with cyclamen that dominate the east lawn. Massed plantings of flowering cherries, barberries, olearias, escallonias, and other wind-resistant shrubs shut off the drive. To the north, *Clematis montana rubens* drapes the towers and crenellations, providing the focal point for a shrubbery of two and a half acres that Lord Talbot planted to link the castle to the walled kitchen garden beyond. Three grass avenues radiate from the castle, with a maze of minor paths between. Entering these is like entering on a voyage of discovery of the plants of the temperate world. Strange hakeas are underplanted with the black-and-green widow iris, *Hermodactylus tuberosus*. *Acanthopanax henryi*, besieged by insects of many kinds when in flower, hangs its giant blackberrylike fruit over spurges and sea hollies, of which Lord Talbot made considerable collections. Groups of olearias, escallonias, hebes, American ceano-

*Malahide Castle*

The Gardens of Ireland

*The terraced beds around the lily pond
contain many of the twenty-eight different
species and cultivars of ceanothus. The
curving yew hedge also shelters a collection
of shrubby potentillas.*

thus (of which there are more than twenty-eight different species and cultivars),
together with others of Lord Talbot's favorite genera, thrive between fine rose
species and carefully selected small trees.

A small green gate provides access to the former kitchen garden, four acres in
extent. Within its walls is now the nucleus of the collection, the Tresco Wall and
the greenhouses. A box-edged path leads south to a willow-hung pond whose surface reflects a neighboring tower. Its sloping sides are thick with trees, shrubs, and
herbaceous plants, including the giant gunnera and the twisted willow from China,
*Salix matsudana* 'Tortuosa'. On the walls of the tower grows *Rosa chinensis mu-
tabilis*, whose flowers change color as they mature, from a coppery flame to a paler
copper, then to pink and, finally, crimson. Nearby is a young tree of the Kashmir
cypress, *Cupressus cashmeriana*, now thought to be extinct in the wild. The collection has spilled over to adjoining areas, the former Rose Garden, the Old Hag-
gard (once a yard for farm animals), and the Chicken Yard. In the first is a
Mediterranean cypress, now forty feet high, up which climbs the rose 'Wedding
Day'. It is surrounded by borders with tender salvias, coronillas, *Rubus lineatus*,
with its unique and beautiful leaves, and a curious form of *Clematis montana* with
serrated edges to its petals.

A collector is fascinated by the unique and curious, the difficult and rare,
adjectives which describe many of the plants gathered by Lord Talbot. Like many

collectors, he maintained meticulous records of all of his plants detailing their origin and performance. These records are now in the possession of the present owner of Malahide, Dublin County Council. Using these, the council has been able to name many of the plants and to learn the secrets of their cultivation. It has also been possible to identify many plants formerly in the collections, and to identify the botanical institutions and gardens to which Lord Talbot sent seed or cuttings of his rarer plants. Thus the council, seeking to restore the collections to their former comprehensiveness, can now ask for seeds or cuttings from the progeny of Lord Talbot's gifts. This vigorous policy of restoration, under the direction of Michael Lynch and Ann James, ensures that the garden at Malahide will in future years continue to be a place of pilgrimage for garden lovers and botanists.

Clematis montana *foams over the boundary of the walled garden.*

The Gardens of Ireland

# Fernhill

• • • • • • • • • • • • • • • • •

COUNTY DUBLIN
Mrs. Sally Walker and Mr. Robert Walker

High in the foothills of the Dublin Mountains and with a wide view over Dublin Bay, the Darley family built the house of Fernhill about 1860. On the hill behind were the limestone quarries that provided much of the building stone for Dublin, and running through the garden of Fernhill was a sunken road down which the carts came carrying the stone to the city below.

The Darleys first planted a shelter belt of Scots pine and larch around their grounds. The shelter belt was particularly thick on the hill behind to break up the prevailing wind, which is from the southwest. (Much of this belt was recently destroyed in a forest fire, which swept down un-

White bluebells act as a foil to the hot colors of mixed azaleas that light up the woods of Scots pine in May.

Preceding pages:
Crevices in the limestone rock were filled with soil to provide homes for plants like Bergenia purpurascens 'Ballawley Hybrid', a form with extra-large leaves and magenta flowers that was produced at the nearby garden of Ballawley Park. As is typical of the natural-looking Robinsonian garden, the cultivated areas merge imperceptibly with the woodland behind.

Viburnum plicatum 'Mariesii', white azalea R. 'Palestrina', and lime-green Euphorbia characias lead the eye to the yellow Banksian rose on the house.

controllably from the mountain behind; its renewal is one of the tasks facing the present owners.)

Below the house, and at some distance from it, as was usual in Ireland, the Darleys made a kitchen garden with box-hedged borders of flowers, but their main contribution to the ornamental garden at Fernhill was the construction of a broad, flat terraced walk on the heights above the house. Like all Victorian garden paths, the walk was extremely wide, so that a group of three ladies in their wide skirts could walk side by side, conversing while they took the afternoon air. As they strolled, they would have enjoyed the views over the bay and, on a clear day, of the Mountains of Mourne, sixty miles to the north. Along either side of the walk young conifers were planted; their sobriety of color was always appealing to the Victorians. Some of these have now reached enormous size. A Scots pine is one of the tallest in the country, and a *Picea smithiana* is so tall it is believed that it must be one of the earliest introductions into this country. Its long weeping branches give it a somewhat funereal air not unappreciated by our grandparents.

Also dating from the Darley period are the magnificent plants of the rhododendron unique to this garden and known as *Rhododendron* 'Fernhill'. It is an *arboreum* hybrid of unknown origin but thought to have been given to Fernhill by Glasnevin Botanic Gardens, Dublin. It grows, eventually, twenty to thirty feet tall and is covered with pinkish flowers in April. The original plant has been propa-

gated, so there are now many plants of different ages in the garden. (This is a good example of the active conservation of a good garden plant at work.)

Fernhill was bought by the Walker family in the 1930s, and it owes its present eminence as a garden to the late Ralph Walker and his wife, Sally. They came to live here about thirty years ago.

Behind the house, the Walkers found what remained of a Victorian rock garden, which was, of course, like all rock gardens of that period, mainly dark and shadowy, a home for a collection of ferns. They cleared it of the overgrowth, letting in light and air so that it could become a modern rock garden with alpines, dwarf bulbs, herbaceous plants, and dwarf sun-loving shrubs. New limestone boulders were brought down from the mountain behind and placed in position next to the natural outcrops of rock. Lastly, a narrow stream was diverted down through the garden in a chain of pools and waterfalls.

Fernhill is now a typical Robinsonian garden. At the time that the house was built, large gardens were subdivided into specialist areas. Trees grew in the arboretum, shrubs in the shrubbery, roses in the rose garden, herbaceous plants in the border, and so on. William Robinson, the proponent of the natural garden, felt that this was artificial. In nature, he argued, trees, shrubs, perennials, and bulbs grow happily side by side and so they should in a garden. In the rock garden at Fernhill, tall cordyline palms or dracaenas, pieris and barberries, rhododen-

*William Robinson argued that in nature trees, shrubs, perennials, and bulbs grow happily side by side, and so they should in a garden. His view is well illustrated by the rock garden at Fernhill. The rich collection of plants includes the wire netting bush, Corokia cotoneaster, whose yellow flowers appear here at center. At this point one looks out over sheltering pine and larch to Dublin Bay and, on a clear day, to the Mourne mountains, sixty miles to the north.*

*Bluebells,* Endymion non-scriptus, *in pink and white as well as in the common blue form, are naturalized in the woodland garden.*

drons and azaleas, perennials, bulbs, rock and water plants all grow together in happy abandon. Each group of plants is allowed to spread or seed itself, just a little, into its neighbor, again to achieve a more natural look. Another of Robinson's dictums was that exotic and native plants should be allowed to mix judiciously together. Not all native plants should be included (many of them we know only too well as weeds), but those that are decorative. In this kind of mix, the exotic plants from foreign lands will look more at home. At Fernhill, there is no barrier between the plants of five continents that grow in the rock garden and the native trees and shrubs of the wood behind. They gradually merge, one into the other.

Ireland has many rhododendron gardens, but not all of them are in as appropriate a site as the one at Fernhill. Rhododendrons are mountain plants. In their native habitats, they tend to grow in open woodland on steepish slopes where they get sharp water drainage off their roots. Also, many of them flower most on top of the plant and so are not seen to advantage in a flat garden where you look up at them. In a steep, downward-sloping garden, where you can look at them from above, they are seen at their best. The sloping woodland at Fernhill, with its litter of rocks tumbled from the hillside above, suits them to perfection. As in many Irish gardens, there is a concentration, on the one hand, of large, large-leaved rhododendron species, and on the other, of tender, often fragrant, species. Of the first, *R. hodgsonii* has a beautiful bark, *R. falconeri* has a rust-colored felt on the underside of its leaves, and *R. sinogrande* has plumes of silvery young foliage to add to the attractions of its large mature leaves. Of the second, *R. lindleyii* has white flowers, *R. edgworthii* white tinted with pink, and *R. dalhousiae* pale yellow flowers to add to the charms of delicious fragrance. Usually the fragrance of these tender rhododendrons can be appreciated only in a greenhouse or conservatory, but at Fernhill, because of the mild climate, it can be experienced in the open air. Like all collectors, the Walkers enjoy the unusual as well as the beautiful. Among the exquisite rhododendrons is *R. genestierianum,* a plant from Upper Burma, with tiny plum-purple flowers that look like large black currants in bud. It is not a beautiful plant, but it is a great curiosity. There is also a small collection of rhododendrons given to Ralph Walker by the Royal Horticultural Society of Ireland on his retirement as president, a post he held for many years.

An enthusiasm for plants often continues unabated. In 1955, Mr. Walker, together with his brother, Philip, purchased the island garden of Rossdohan in County Kerry as a holiday home, taking on its care in addition to the twenty-acre garden at Fernhill. Rossdohan had been famous at the end of the last century for the successful growing of plants from the Australian continent, but it had become derelict. The Walkers set about restoring it, clearing away overgrowth, giving the old trees and shrubs light and air, and setting out new plantings. At Rossdohan, eucalyptus, tree ferns, the Australian blackwood acacia (*Acacia melanoxylon*), the Australian muskwood (*Olearia argophylla*), and the lily-of-the-valley tree (*Clethra arborea*) from sunny Madeira all seed themselves around parent plants as they do in their native homelands. It is not surprising that the Walkers dug up some of these seedlings and brought them to Fernhill to see how they would survive in the somewhat harsher climate of the east coast. Now, in the shelter of the rhododendron wood, you can see young and semimature plants seldom seen around Dublin except in greenhouses and conservatories.

In contrast to the wildness of the rhododendron wood is another survivor from the Victorian garden at Fernhill—a laurel lawn. In the nineteenth century, com-

*The Gardens of Ireland*

Magnolia x wilsonii.

mon laurel (*Prunus laurocerasus*) supplanted holly as the most popular under-planting for woodland groves. Laurel spreads so rapidly that it often runs out of control, but our grandparents kept it in bounds by clipping it back every year to a flat, table-top level—what was known as a laurel lawn. The one at Fernhill is one of the few in Ireland surviving from those days.

On the lawn and in the sloping field in front of the house bloom many thousands of daffodils in spring. They are the old varieties that seed themselves more freely than the newly bred ones and so, over many years, they have spread into natural-looking groups. When they flower with the cherries along the driveway to the house the effect is otherworldly. A little later in the season, sheets of bluebells, which again have been allowed to seed freely, flower under the trees around the lawns. The common blue is mixed with clumps of the white and pink varieties to give a dreamlike haze of soft color in the dappled shade of the trees. The bulb theme is continued in autumn when a mass of colchicums (often referred to as autumn crocus) flower pink under the spreading branches of a sweet chestnut tree.

At some distance down the slope from the house is the traditional kitchen garden, divided by a pair of paths crossing at the center. Down either side of the paths flowers are grown for cutting, backed by apple trees trained on wire espaliers. Behind, in the four quarters, the vegetables and soft fruit are grown in regular rows. Some space is traditionally stolen in Irish kitchen gardens for a small design

*The shadows of an old sweet chestnut fall across the lawn in front of the picturesque and much-extended Victorian house.*

of box-edged beds in which cutting roses are grown. The box hedges hide the generally unsightly ankles of hybrid tea and floribunda roses. Among them, the Walkers now grow a small collection of old Irish hybrid teas like 'Irish Elegance' and 'Irish Sensation'. These were bred before the First World War by Dicksons of Hawlmark in County Down, still among the best rose breeders in Europe. Many of their old varieties have been presumed lost until, occasionally, one is unexpectedly found in an old garden. 'Irish Fireflame', for example, bred by them in 1913, was recently found growing in the Dublin garden of Miss Frances-Jane French.

The last gardens made by the Walkers are the heather bank and the stream garden. The heather bank juts out of the rock garden near the house and provides glowing winter color within sight of the windows. One striking feature is the way in which the cultivars of winter heath (*Erica carnea*), flowering in white and many shades of pink, have been interplanted with groups of *Bergenia purpurascens*, whose large, leathery crimson leaves contrast with the minuscule leaves of the heathers. One of the bergenias with especially large leaves is the famous 'Ballawley Hybrid', bred at Ballawley Park, near Fernhill.

One of the characteristics of the Robinsonian wild garden is that the design is not predetermined in relation to the house but is developed from any natural features that occur on the garden site, even if these bear no relationship to the house, and even if they are out of sight of the house. At some distance from the house at Fernhill, and out of sight of it, is a stream flowing down from the mountains. The Walkers seized on it as an opportunity for making a water garden. The stream bed was widened and small dams constructed to make pools and waterfalls. At one point a bridge was constructed. In one of the pools an island was made. The bones of the water garden were in place. Then they began to plant it. Skunk cabbages, rodgersias, astilbes, and other water-margin plants make streams of color along the banks. Candelabra primulas of many species and varieties, ferns, periwinkles, pulmonarias, and blue-eyed Mary star the ground with many colors. Nearby is one of the outstanding features of the garden and the special interest of Mrs. Walker—a collection of primulas. Here are auriculas, polyanthuses, and numerous other primroses thriving in the light shade and moist ground. To keep the colony happy, the clumps must be lifted, divided, and replanted in fresh soil or position every second year. Otherwise the ground becomes what is known as "primula-sick." This is a considerable labor, carried out by Mrs. Walker already many times, but the value of doing so increases every year as fewer and fewer people grow extensive collections because of the labor involved.

Ralph Walker died in 1980 and since then the garden has been managed by Sally Walker, who has enriched its planting and opened it to the public during every week of the season. She works hard, especially as she refuses to use a simazine weed killer in the shrubberies, finding the bare patches of soil it leaves between the shrubs unsightly. Mulches of leaf mold and farmyard manure are used to enrich the soil, particularly on the primula and rhododendron beds. They harbor slugs and snails, of course, but Mrs. Walker believes that because she does not use weed killer there is a big population of birds around that feed on the snails and slugs, and nature's balance is maintained. She is helped by an experienced and skillful gardener, Austin McCleery, once head gardener at Malahide Castle, who comes two days a week, and another gardener who has been part of Fernhill for many years and who does a considerable amount of the heavy work of clearing, felling, and moving trees and shrubs that is necessary in a garden of this size.

Mrs. Walker's son, Robert, has established a successful nursery at the entrance

to the garden. He began by raising herbs to supply the newly sophisticated Irish dinner table and has now branched out into a general list of trees, shrubs, and perennials, concentrating on those that visitors may have seen and liked on their tour in the garden.

Both garden and nursery thrive through their close proximity to Dublin, with its large population, and the city in its turn profits from the skill, imagination, and labor of the Walker family in maintaining their garden and opening it to the public. Garden parties for charities, outdoor sculpture exhibitions, and other events help to bring people into the garden who might not normally visit it and, one hopes, new devotees of the art of gardening are born.

*The screen of tall conifers along the Victorian terrace walk provides a green background for a well-spaced planting of* Pieris formosa, *with its red young foliage and creamy-white flowers, a purple Japanese maple, and the* Rhododendron arboreum *hybrid 'Fernhill', which has just finished flowering.*

The Gardens of Ireland

# Berkeley Forest

· · · · · · · · · · · · · · · · ·

**COUNTY WEXFORD**
Count and Countess Gunnar Bernstorff

Berkeley Forest, where Count and Countess Bernstorff live and farm, was named, it is thought, for the grandfather of the famous eighteenth-century Irish philosopher George Berkeley. Countess Bernstorff is a painter. This gives her garden a special interest because it is evident that she looks at plants from a pictorial, as well as a horticultural, point of view.

The house lies in a shallow bowl of beech trees. Sheep graze in the parkland against a backdrop of the distant Blackstairs Mountains. An old oak presides over a thick shrubbery that shelters the house. On a slope to the west, within walls of faded brick, lies the garden.

In the walled garden, tall columnar conifers such as Chamaecyparis lawsoniana 'Columnaris' are used as green-pillared gateways between different parts of the garden, while lower-growing, feathery conifers like Chamaecyparis pisifera 'Plumosa Rogersii' are used to give body and texture in the shrub borders.

Preceding pages:
Sheep graze in the parkland, which lies in a shallow bowl of beech trees with a backdrop of the distant Blackstairs Mountains.

A thick shrubbery envelops and shelters the late Georgian house.

It is entered through a small enclosure that acts as a lobby to the main garden and has been developed as an outdoor fernery. A white-painted garden seat in Gothic style is set against a wall which Countess Bernstorff has stencilled with a simple but striking design in Gothic tracery. It is a deft exercise in scenography, turning inarticulate space into eloquent garden theater.

For most gardens the house is the focal point; but when the garden is at some distance from the house, as at Beaulieu, or has its back turned awkwardly to it, as at Berkeley Forest, another focal point must be supplied. This the Bernstorffs have done by building a thatched summerhouse at the top of the garden, the pitch of the roof designed to echo the fall of the ground. The roof's pointed shape is also reflected in the Gothic windows and in the pointed tips of the many dwarf conifers planted around. This composition of lines and pointed shapes reveals the owner's pictorial sensibility. (Countess Bernstorff's next project is to turn the interior into a shell grotto like those that graced many seventeenth-century gardens.) The windows of the summerhouse are painted dark blue, harmonizing with the blue tones of the flowers chosen for its vicinity. On either side grows a silver birch, which, in autumn, sheds leaves of pale gold onto the paler gold of the thatch. Thus the area recreates in miniature the thatched summerhouses in the birch groves of Denmark, Count Bernstorff's native land.

The harmony in blue around the summerhouse is rare in Ireland, for most Irish gardens rely on red as their principal color—it is, after all, complementary to the

Curving hydrangea borders and pools of silvery lamb's ears and artemisia lead the eye to the thatched summerhouse at the top of the garden. The blue of delphiniums and ceanothus echoes the paintwork of the summerhouse windows.

country's traditional green. At Berkeley Forest, however, clumps of the Californian shrub *Ceanothus impressus*, with its tiny evergreen leaves and myriads of deep blue flowers, give vivid displays in spring. These are succeeded by, and sometimes happily overlap with, a multitude of tall blue delphiniums, all requiring regular division and stout staking to keep them at their peak. These, in turn, are followed in summer by groves of mop-head hydrangeas, their flowers a dense blue on account of the acidity of the soil. Upright pairs of blue-green conifers like *Chamaecyparis lawsoniana* 'Columnaris' and *C. l.* 'Fletcheri Nana' provide sombre accents. Tight-knit clumps of blue bellflowers, *Campanula persicifolia*, and blue-leaved hostas such as *Hosta sieboldiana elegans* underline the basic theme. The composition is completed by carpets of self-sown forget-me-nots and hand-sown violas covering the ground in large numbers.

As blue does not show well against dark green, the success of a blue garden depends, as Countess Bernstorff knows, on the use of silver foliage. So, at Berkeley Forest, there are huge mounds of *Artemisia arborescens*, its finely divided leaves of the lightest silver, and clumps of *Senecio cineraria* 'Candicans', of a similar silver, around their base. Woollier grays are furnished by the foliage of *Anaphalis yedoensis*, lamb's ears, and the purple sage, *Salvia officinalis* 'Tricolor'. The gray leaves of the last are margined with cream and its young growth tinted with purple, a hue taken up in a nearby hebe. The metallic silvers of *Hebe pinguifolia* 'Pagei' and *Ruta graveolens* 'Jackman's Blue' add an icier note. Countess Bernstorff does

*A theatrical corner—Gothic vaulting traced on a wall by Countess Bernstorff and an antique cast-iron seat decorate an outdoor fernery.*

Mahonia japonica, *like most mahonias, produces the most richly colored foliage in soil that has been improved by the addition of leaf mold and peat.*

not like plants that combine yellow flowers with silver foliage, so that many commonly used silver-foliaged shrubs like senecio, santolina, and helichrysum are excluded. Unfortunately, those chosen are often semitender and have to be replaced after a hard winter's frost.

Through hydrangea hedges, which turn a ravishing mixture of blue, maroon, purple, and brown as the leaves fade and the flowers run to seed, steps descend to a semicircular lawn. Here stand Victorian chairs and a table with a samovar, always ready for the arrival of a party for tea.

More steps descend between a pair of Lawson cypress, which have grown so large that Countess Bernstorff contemplates their removal and replacement by a smaller pair. The lower lawn is bounded with a hedge of the white rugosa rose 'Blanc Double de Coubert', above which can be seen a wide panorama of park and mountain. The surrounding borders are remarkable for their use of dwarf conifers among the shrubs. Dwarf conifers are too often used like vegetable gnomes, their curious shapes often bullying the eye to attention, but at Berkeley Forest, two types are used to perfection. Tall, conical ones make green-pillared gateways—a variety of Lawson cypress, the Alberta spruce (*Picea glauca albertiana* 'Conica'), and the Irish juniper (*Juniperus communis hibernica*) are used in this way. Low, spreading conifers, on the other hand, are mixed in the borders in a painterly fashion, to give body and texture to the other plantings. Feathery dwarf Japanese cedars

*The garden lies on a west-facing slope to the rear of the house. Tall Lawson cypress in variety lend permanence to the shorter-lived plantings of cistus and broom, lamb's ears, and* Rosa rugosa *'Blanc Double de Coubert.'*

(*Cryptomeria japonica* 'Nana'), Savin junipers (*Juniperus sabina* 'Tamariscifolia'), and Sawara cypresses (*Chamaecyparis pisifera* 'Boulevard') give low hummocks of foliage, while the taller Sawara cypresses, *Chamaecyparis pisifera* 'Plumosa Aurea' and 'Squarrosa', provide loose backgrounds. Many of them have richly colored winter coats, their foliage turning a warm bronze or a blue- or even yellow-green.

Among the conifers, Countess Bernstorff has planted clumps of those hebes, potentillas, helianthemums, and shrub roses that flower in pastel shades only. No rich reds or yellows are allowed to interrupt her pale color flow, and the brown stems and seed heads of the potentillas harmonize in winter with the bronze-brown of the cryptomerias.

A pool has recently been made to one side of the summerhouse, its mellow brick edges overhung by blue ceanothus. Behind is an iron field gate, an excellent example of the craftsmanship of an old Irish blacksmith. It is an appropriate focal point for this area, for the Bernstorffs have long been collectors and supporters of traditional Irish country crafts.

A painter uses pigment to define form on a canvas. Here, Countess Bernstorff has used plants to create a number of garden spaces, each with a different color harmony.

*The Gardens of Ireland*

# Kilmokea House

· · · · · · · · · · · · · · · · ·

COUNTY WEXFORD
Mr. and Mrs. David Price

The subtropical gardens of Ireland lie mainly along the western coast-line. It is a surprise, therefore, to find Kilmokea on the eastern sea-board. It lies, however, on Great Island, a large peninsula about five miles from the sea on Waterford Harbour, and being surrounded on three sides by tidal water, it enjoys a mild microclimate. Here, many of the plants familiar to visitors to the great gardens of the west, Ilnacullin, Glenveagh, and Derreen, grow happily and rapidly.

Kilmokea House is a tall Georgian rectory built in 1794. When Mr. and Mrs. David Price came to live here thirty-five years ago, it was surrounded by a billowing sea of laurel. At the back was a derelict kitchen garden and a disused cemetery.

*The paved pool garden with the fountain of a leaden faun.*

*Preceding pages:*
*The late-flowering* Magnolia quinquepeta *'Nigra' has a vase-shaped flower, which is dark, vinous purple without but paler within.*

*Pink clematis and rock roses echo the warm tints of the stone and paintwork of the house, while clipped yew cones and a simple lawn set off its classical lines.*

Today, all is changed. A short drive under fine beech trees leads up to the old glebe house. To the left of the drive, the Prices have planted spring borders. Flowering cherries, drimys, pittosporums, and olearias grow out of loose carpets of daffodils and blue-eyed Mary. To the right, summer borders succeed. They are planted mainly in a color scheme of reds. Old shrub roses like *Rosa x highdownensis*, 'Sarah van Fleet', and *moyesii* and its form 'Geranium', and red leptospermums, *Leptospermum scoparium* 'Nichollsii' and 'Red Damask' grow above a border of red *Lobelia tupa*.

Opposite the entrance to the house is a garden enclosed by a holly hedge. Its entrance is guarded by a pair of stone peacocks sculpted by the English artist Simon Verity. They announce one of the features of the garden as a whole: its birds. Peacocks, fantail pigeons, ducks, and rooks all contribute a cacophony of sound as well as ornament to the grounds. This little enclosed garden is designed to focus on an urn made by the English firm of Chilstone; it is a copy of the one the eighteenth-century English poet and garden designer Alexander Pope had made for his garden at Twickenham outside London. The layout is completed with a variety of ferns, hostas, and bergenias giving good foliage and textural contrasts in the cool shade of the hedges.

Around the side of the house is the sheltered dovecote garden. Being enclosed, it provides a good place to grow the very tender jasmine *Jasminum polyanthum* in

its double form and early camellias, without their flowers being spoiled by the cold. In the middle, on raised and gravelled beds, grow alpines, heathers, and dwarf conifers—small plants to fit the scale of a small garden. A pencillike Irish juniper (*Juniperus communis* 'Hibernica') contrasts effectively with the low, horizontal lines of the beds.

Behind the house, where once the kitchen garden of the rectory stood, is a big and open lawn that sets off the fine proportions of the house. Too many plants here would have competed for interest with its architecture. The only decoration is a variety of figures shaped in sombre yew, their rounded forms contrasting nicely with the severe lines of the house. Flat-topped tables, cones, and cylinders abound. Mr. Price's experience of topiary has taught him that you cannot set out to make it into a predetermined shape: you have to watch carefully which way the tree itself wants to grow and then follow it with the shears.

On the left, looking out from the house, is a border of lupins along the edge of the lawn. A long lupin border such as this is not often seen now, as the Russell hybrids, which are available in a wonderful range of colors, are not long-lived, needing propagation every third year.

On the right-hand side of the lawn, to balance the lupin border, Mrs. Price has made a herbaceous border, which is her special care. Each year, under her tutelage, a midsummer haze of soft blues emerges in groups of tall delphiniums, an-

*The gateway out of the walled garden into the wild garden is approached through a mass of the lime-green flowers of lady's mantle, which acts as an edging for the rose borders.*

*Overleaf:*
*The scarlet red of* Lychnis chalcedonica *wanders through golden loosestrife. Behind the softer colors of campanula, thalictrum, and the rambling rose 'Albertine' recede.*

The Gardens of Ireland

*The stream and woodland garden David Price has made during the last twenty-five years.*

chusas, and campanulas. They are accompanied by the pale yellows of clumps of yarrows, ligularias, and golden loosestrife. This blue-and-yellow color scheme is enriched by spots of red and pink from lychnis, heucheras, and penstemons, their hot color being cooled by well-spaced silver foliage.

Behind these borders on either side of the lawn are a series of garden "rooms." One is an iris garden enclosed by a hedge of purple plum. Irises bloom luxuriantly for a short time each year and are otherwise dull, so it is a good idea to have them in an enclosed garden where they may be visited and enjoyed when in bloom and then languish out of sight for the remainder of the year. Another is a vegetable garden carefully laid out on a regular plan.

Chief among these side gardens, however, is the paved pool garden. The pool surface is broken by the steady stream from a fountain—a leaden faun, copied from one still working in the excavated gardens of Pompeii. Low, spreading conifers soften the hard lines of the paving. A *Magnolia x soulangiana* throws welcome shade. Steps lead up to a neoclassical temple and, in early summer, the cracks between the paving stones are set alight with the brilliant reds, whites, and pinks of self-sown valerian. In Ireland, valerian is often seen growing in the cracks of old garden walls where it is generally, despite its brilliance of flower, regarded as a weed. It was Mr. Price's happy idea to allow it to self-seed in his paving.

The transformation of the old rectory kitchen garden into a central lawn flanked on either side by a suite of garden rooms is in the classic modern mode.

The impact of a formal garden is enhanced if it is set in contrast with an informal or wild one. Similarly, the impact of a sun-filled garden is enhanced by its contrast with a shady one. The Prices have achieved both these effects by developing a small woodland garden outside the walls of the original rectory garden. It is laid out around an old horse pond, the light reflected off its surface providing a bright focal point amidst the shadowy oak and beech around. The Prices have made it interesting by planting a giant-leaved gunnera by the water's edge, a swamp cypress, mimosa (*Acacia dealbata*), and a couple of Chilean fire bushes (*Embothrium coccineum*).

It comes as a surprise to visitors that these are not all of Kilmokea gardens, for across the public road is another and newer garden on what used to be a boggy slope. Twenty years ago, Mr. Price decided to make it into a woodland garden, despite the fact there were no trees. An unlikely project, you might think, but its present luxuriance demonstrates how a woodland garden can be made from scratch in a relatively short time.

Mr. Price's first step was to plant a grid of trees at six-foot centers over the entire area of four acres. For this, he chose a rich mixture of conifers: Japanese larch (*Larix kaempferi*), Douglas fir (*Pseudotsuga menziesii*), Sitka spruce (*Picea sitchensis*), and Western hemlock (*Tsuga heterophylla*). Vigorous trees, their thick canopies would in time provide shelter from the winds that blow off the estuary.

The second stage of the development of the woodland garden could now begin.

*Candelabra primulas lead the eye into the dark recesses of the woodland garden, while magnolia blossom and variegated dogwood light up the foreground.*

*Candelabra primula*, Primula japonica.

*The Gardens of Ireland*

At the upper end of the slope was a particularly wet area, which Mr. Price suspected was once a pond. He determined to revive it. With earth-moving machinery he began to dig, and, to his surprise, the remains of an old horizontal wooden mill and millstone were revealed. Further excavation uncovered evidence that the present pool is at the center of what was a large, double-ramparted Viking trading post. A concrete dam was built at the lower end of the new pool. Over it the water spills into a chain of linked pools and falls, running down through the center of the garden, acting as its focal point and axis. Field-drains were let into this water system to soak up any excess ground moisture remaining. The infrastructure of the new woodland garden was complete.

Only then, after some ten years, did Mr. Price commence the ornamental planting, the third stage in the development. As the conifer wood grew, he made clearings in which to plant some ornamental trees, whose growth has been very rewarding. Scarlet oaks are now about forty-five feet, the plum-fruited yew (*Podocarpus andinus*) fifty-five feet, and the manna or ribbon gum (*Eucalyptus viminalis*) sixty-five feet. He planted unusual hedges of the South American lantern tree (*Crinodenron hookeranum*), the Tasmanian mountain pepper (*Drimys lanceolata*), and the Chinese bamboo (*Arundinaria nitida*). Already the rich palette that a mild climate puts at the disposal of the Irish gardener is evident.

Many great Irish gardens have famous collections of big rhododendrons but Kilmokea, by contrast, is interesting for its collection of smaller and dwarf species.

*On either side of the central lawn is an intricate arrangement of garden rooms. That to the west includes a paved pool garden and a herbaceous border, beyond which can be seen the old cemetery and Waterford harbor, this large body of water ensuring that the garden enjoys a mild microclimate.*

*Opposite page:*
*Birds—peacocks, fantail pigeons, rooks, and ducks—add life and ornament to the gardens at Kilmokea.*

*The colors of golden loosestrife,* Lysimachia punctata, *red* Lychnis chalcedonica *, and silver Scotch thistle are clearly discernible against the dark background of yew hedge.*

In the half-shade of the wood, the low domes of *R. yakusnimanum* and *williamsianum* glow when in bloom. There are curiosities like *R. spinuliferum*, whose flowers narrow rather than unfold at the mouth. There is the tender, scented rhododendron of local interest, *R. burmanicum*, which was discovered in Burma and brought to Europe by Lady Wheeler Cuffe of neighboring County Kilkenny.

A garden full of rare plants has, of course, an inestimable value of its own, but a garden full of the same plants obtained not from nurseries but by gift or purchase from great and famous gardens takes on a further value of association with them— rather as the provenance of the works of art adds interest to an art collection. Mr. Price is well aware of this. So many of his plants have been brought from the great gardens of the south coast of Ireland. From Fota come South African watsonias, from Derreen tree ferns, from Glanleam in County Kerry the variegated myrtle *Myrtus apiculata* 'Glanleam Gold'. The latter now forms the basis of a collection of fourteen kinds of myrtle that is unique in Ireland and which is augmented by related species such as *Syzygium paniculatum*. Moreover, there is no greater reminder of your native land than a plant characteristic of its landscape or gardens. Mrs. Price is Scottish and so enjoys many of the plants obtained from the great subtropical gardens of the west coast of Scotland—rhododendrons from Brodick on the Isle of Arran, and echiums from the Royal Botanic Gardens at Logan on the Mull of Galloway.

A collection of plants does not, however, make a garden unless the plants are grouped to aesthetic effect. Mr. Price has used foliage to create such effect in two different ways, both as a background for the display of flowers and as a feature of interest in itself. The leaves of gunnera, hostas, and the weeping birch *Betula pendula* 'Youngii' act as backgrounds for the drifts of candelabra primulas along the banks of the stream. The foliage of other plants is used as a striking feature in itself: *Populus candicans* (or *balsamifera*) 'Aurora', with its green-and-white blotched leaf; *Cornus controversa* 'Variegata', its form reminiscent of a pirouetting ballerina, and *Azara microphylla variegata*, with tiny mustard-and-green leaves that originated in the old County Cork garden of Belgrove.

The garden as a whole is seven acres in size and is maintained by the Prices with the assistance of only one student gardener. Its maintenance is eased, however, by Mr. Price's thorough knowledge of modern weed killers and the use of simazine, in particular, in the woodland area. Although this initially leaves much bare soil between the plants, mosses eventually emerge in its wake and Mr. Price is encouraging these to spread and so form a green carpet over the beds. Although many prefer not to use chemical weed killers to this extent, their use here has enabled these dedicated gardeners to create, within a relatively short space of time, and maintain a garden and plant collection of beauty and consequence.

*The scarlet trumpet honeysuckle,* Lonicera sempervirens, *needs a warm wall in a mild area. Here it grows above a border of hardy geraniums and hypericum, the latter's yellow being echoed in the golden ivy,* Hedera helix *'Buttercup'.*

# Lucy's Wood

• • • • • • • • • • • • • • • •

COUNTY WEXFORD
Miss Evelyn Booth

The smallest of the gardens in this book, Lucy's Wood is the creation of a botanist, Miss Evelyn Booth. The garden, made over a period of thirty years, is behind her house, a traditional Irish farmhouse on the edge of Bunclody, a small town in County Wexford.

Wildflowers collected by her on her botanizing expeditions grow side by side with more familiar garden plants. She has always fought (in a gentle way) for a better recognition of the contribution wildflowers can make to the garden. This has gone against the modern trend of breeding new plants with brighter color, but Miss Booth maintains that wild plants have a delicacy and naturalness denied to the new-bred hybrids.

*Lucy's Wood*

An old China rose flowers at the same time as a powder-blue ceanothus; the combination is completed characteristically by a wild plant, a delicate erect thistle from southern Europe, Galactites tomentosa.

Preceding pages:
Under a silver willow-leaved pear, white narcissi nod in the breeze.

The long gravel path leading from the trelliswork porch is typical of the traditional Irish cottage garden, rapidly disappearing today. Behind the Escallonia 'Apple Blossom', a hybrid bred in Northern Ireland by the Slieve Donard nursery, is the vertical line of an Irish yew.

Now, with the present concern for ecology and conservation, she is finding her long-standing approach to be the height of fashion.

For many years, Miss Booth has been the recognized expert on the wildflowers of her neighboring county of Carlow, and in 1979, she listed them and their distribution in her book *The Flora of County Carlow*. It was the first Irish flora published since 1950, the first of an inland county, and the first written by a woman. In her introduction, she acknowledges her debt to a long line of Irish botanists, but particularly to Miss Barton and Miss Rawlins, friends and amateur botanists in whose footsteps she continues. Needlework and flower arranging, two other favored pursuits of women of her generation, are also great interests of Miss Booth. Her house is full of examples of her prowess as a needlewoman, and her artful arrangements of dried and fresh garden flowers are found everywhere in her house, precursors of the garden behind. There is a delightful unity of purpose here.

The garden is laid out like a traditional cottage garden—a type rapidly disappearing in the Ireland of today. The back door and trelliswork porch lead onto a long gravel path bordered with flowers. Behind these is a cornucopia of flowers, vegetables, and fruit. Bird tables ensure the presence of many feathered creatures to mop up the slugs and snails. Over the garden fence is the neighboring working farm. Lucy's Wood is the realization of that rural idyll of which many of us dream.

The ideal site for a garden is one that slopes up from the house, so you can see the plants rising in tiers before you. Behind the house at Lucy's Wood the ground slopes in this ideal way and Miss Booth has made a rock bank of it. The rocks are of white quartzite, brought down from the nearby Blackstairs Mountains. Here is another lesson for the garden maker—the use of local stone will enable a new garden to fit into its surroundings. Once the rockwork terraces were in place, Miss Booth felt the need to break up their long horizontal lines by introducing a vertical feature. She chose three Irish junipers (*Juniperus communis* 'Hibernica'). Common juniper grows wild in the west of Ireland, but the origin of the upright, pencilike form known as the Irish juniper is unknown. It is one of the best of the columnar dwarf conifers, but it tends to open out of its narrow habit with age, and often, as at Lucy's Wood, has to be tied up with wire at that stage.

At the bottom of the bank, nearest the house, is a network of tiny plants. It is necessary to get down on your knees if you are not to miss these treasures. (Lucy's Wood is a garden in which close visual contact with the tiny plants is essential.) Conspicuous among them is a rare form of the Irish shamrock, *Trifolium repens* (Atropurpureum). Its leaves are purple rather than the usual green. If Miss Booth has a wildflower in her garden, the chances are that it is a rare rather than a common form. But her choice of plants for her garden is not based on botanical rarity alone. As she is a keen arranger of flowers, color is important to her, too. The purple shamrock is just one of the threads of a tapestry in which the purple stems and flowers of that unusual member of the Lily family, *Ophiopogon planiscapus nigrescens*, the dark *Geranium nigricans*, the dwarf purple barberry, *Berberis thunbergii* 'Maximowiczii', and the larger one, *Berberis thunbergii* 'Atropurpurea', are also interwoven. Associated with the last in a striking color combination is a double pink rambler rose grown from a cutting from a rose Miss Booth spotted in a cottage garden over thirty years ago. As a contrast to the purple hues, a silver planting theme has also been established. The soft and very silky leaves of silverweed (*Potentilla anserina*) mix with silvery *Geranium argenteum* and *Hieracium villosum* and with more common plants like artemisias and hebes.

On the walls of the house grows an old pink China rose that flowers at the same time as a powder-blue ceanothus beneath. The combination is completed characteristically by a wild plant: the delicate, erect thistle *Galactites*, with silvery stems and lilac flowers, which has been allowed to seed itself in the gravel next to the ceanothus. Botanists, of course, have always been interested in grasses and rushes as well as flowers. So near the thistle is a silvery clump of the snowy woodrush (*Luzula nivea*).

In the greenhouse, the sunny benches are filled with pots of geraniums and plumbago, and an extraordinary, unnamed aeonium that looks, when about to flower, like nothing more than a vegetable Viking helmet. In the shadows are ferns, including the Killarney fern (*Trichomanes speciosum*) and the maidenhair fern (*Adiantum*), long the pride of many cottage windowsills in Ireland.

Going around Miss Booth's garden with her, you are struck by the fact that she rarely, if ever, announces that she got a plant in a nursery or garden center. They have all been given to her by a network of gardening friends, or she has begged them from gardens visited or from roadside gardens seen on her botanizing expeditions. As she is also a keen fisherwoman, her long days on the riverbank have yielded many native plants to decorate her garden. Some of the gifts have been unexpected. She recalls how her red columbine, *Aquilegia coccinea*, arrived hid-

*Botanists have always been interested as much in grasses and rushes as in flowers.*

*Wildflowers grow side by side with more familiar garden plants. The native perennial pennywort,* Umbilicus rupestris, *is seen here with the almost black leaves of* Liriope planiscapus *'Nigrescens', a member of the lily family.*

*Opposite page:*
*The swordlike leaves of purple Australian flax are threaded with the tiny flowerheads of self-sown violets.*

den in the trunk of a visitor's car. He did not want it to be seen until he had checked that Miss Booth's garden was good enough to have it. Gardeners do not give their treasures away lightly.

Miss Booth now talks of a future time when she will not be able to look after her own plants. Her garden is one in which the tiny detail is all, detail that requires her daily ministrations—weeding, dividing, staking, and pruning. It is a fragile creation, one that will not long survive neglect. She hopes that the garden will be broken up with care, and that, like the man who arrived with the red columbine, she will find good homes for her treasured plants. Even if her garden is broken up, its philosophy of combining garden and wild plants will live in the minds and gardens of those who have seen Lucy's Wood and been influenced by its gentle but learned character.

*The Gardens of Ireland*

# Killruddery

· · · · · · · · · · · · · · · · ·

COUNTY WICKLOW
Lord and Lady Ardee

Killruddery can claim to be the oldest garden in Ireland. It can also claim to be one of the most important. However, it takes a considerable effort of the historical imagination to appreciate it fully, for since the time it was laid out our ideas of what constitutes a garden have changed. For us, a garden is a private domain, a retreat from the world, but Killruddery was laid out in the time of Louis XIV and in the French style. The gardens at Versailles and other great French chateaux were rather like our public parks. They were conceived and designed to accommodate hundreds of courtiers, even in carriages; their avenues, paths, terraces, and flights of steps were correspondingly large, and the whole garden was on a grand scale.

*This winged figure, made by the German firm of Kahl of Potsdam, is part of an extensive collection of Victorian garden statuary at Killruddery.*

*Preceding pages:*
*The conservatory's principal window overlooks the parterre designed as its setting.*

*The conservatory was built in 1852 to a design by the Scottish architect William Burn.*

A further difference lies in the manner in which gardens were used. Nowadays, we think of gardens as areas in which we enjoy growing and looking at ornamental plants, but before cinema and television, when social life was more centered in the home, gardens also played an important role in entertainment. In the seventeenth and eighteenth centuries, and even in the nineteenth, an outdoor theater, a bowling green, and a pond for boating were, for example, considered essential features of any important garden. It was also vital to provide food for the table, and there would be separate kitchen gardens and orchards, duck decoys and fish ponds. All of these features once graced Killruddery and many still survive.

The estate of Killruddery was granted to Sir William Brabazon, later to become the first earl of Meath, in 1618. His house was destroyed in the Civil War in 1645, a time when many Irish noblemen went into exile in France. There they became familiar with Versailles and the other great formal gardens of the time, and when they returned to Ireland they brought with them a newfound taste for the French garden style. By 1682, the fourth earl of Meath had begun to lay out a new garden at Killruddery and two years later, the noted surveyor Sir William Petty noted ruefully in his diary that his gardener of twelve years' standing had gone to the earl of Meath at Killruddery. The gardener, Bonet, or Bonnet, is thought to have been French and responsible for the design of the formal garden we see today.

About eighteen acres were walled in to the south of the new house, thought to have been constructed between 1651 and 1675. The enclosed area was then divided into three parts; the two outer ones were heavily planted with trees, but the central one, in front of the house, was left open. In it were sunk a pair of canals, 550 feet long and occupying about two-thirds of the whole area. They act as mirrors to the sky. Linking them to the house were box parterres, no longer existing.

The section to the east of the canals was further subdivided into three sections known respectively as The Labyrinth, "The Angles," and The Bowling Green. The Labyrinth, of course, was designed to provide people with the amusement of getting lost within its high hedges. "The Angles" were angled walks, also enclosed by high hedges, that crossed and recrossed each other, their intersections marked by classical statues. Groups of friends could walk, meet, and separate, and then have the pleasure of meeting and separating again. The use of different materials for the hedges of the Angles gives variety to the design—yew for the outer hedges, hornbeam for the inner ones, and lime for the central walk. The effect is bewitching on a bright May day when the leaves are still freshly green. Beyond is the Bowling Green, which consists of a sunken lawn surrounded by high grass terraces from which to view the progress of the game. It is worth remembering that the origins of our modern lawn lie in the seventeenth-century bowling green, when selected grass seed was first used to ensure a true roll of the ball.

The area to the west of the canals is likewise subdivided into three parts, known as "The Wilderness," "The Beech Circle," and "The Sylvan Theatre." The Wilderness, which occupies most of the area, is not a wilderness in the sense with which we are familiar today. In the French style, a Wilderness might simply be a part of the garden without clipped hedges. That at Killruddery is composed of straight avenues under lime trees focusing on classical statues set in the woodland clearings. At the end of the main avenue is the Beech Circle. Sixty feet in diameter, it is enclosed by double beech hedges thirty feet high. Within the double hedges is a dark tunnel, with windowlike openings at intervals, where people might walk in the shade during a hot summer's day. The center of the circle is, surprisingly, almost entirely occupied by a circular pond ornamented with fountains in the

*The Gardens of Ireland*

shape of putti and dolphins. Louis XIV had introduced such figures into the garden at Versailles in order to counteract the solemnity of statues of mythological and classical figures with ones depicting the joys of youth. Nearby is the Sylvan Theatre, which is hidden within high hedges of bay laurel. Inside are semicircular rows of grass banks on which the audience sits and a grass stage flanked by stone deities.

This was the extent of the original seventeenth-century garden at Killruddery. Fifty years later, there was another burst of activity. The walls around the garden were taken down and the whole composition extended into the landscape with a Lime Avenue, now one of the finest in Ireland. A water staircase was also made to one side of the main vista. Its cascades descended to a pond known as The Ace of Clubs on account of its shape, but this is no longer visible.

Lady Meath, the wife of the sixth earl, was devoted to flowers, and her lists of them, together with bills for their purchase, are still preserved at Killruddery. It is fascinating to read which flowers were grown over two hundred and fifty years ago. In 1731, for example, there was a payment to a Mr. Bacon for pineapples, trees, and carnations (thirty-one different carnations are listed under Mr. Bacon's name). No less than seventy-four Irish varieties of auricula and sixty-nine English ones are noted in 1736. Three years later Lady Meath lists tulips and ranunculus from Holland and tulips from Lille and Brussels. In 1754, she orders hyacinths from Haarlem and Leyden. Unfortunately, no trace of her garden has been found.

*The planting of the Victorian box parterre has been modernized by the use of lavender and yellow lily-flowered tulips instead of the traditional spring bedding.*

*Stone balustrading designed by Daniel Robertson, architect of the nearby garden of Powerscourt, encloses the forecourt and the stable clock tower.*

*Opposite page:*
*The view from the natural rock garden over the house, its sheltering woods, and the Sugar Loaf mountain beyond.*

*Twin canals, 550 feet long, act as mirrors to the sky and lead the eye to the double lime avenue and park.*

It is remarkable that this old garden at Killruddery has survived so many changes of fashion, especially when the house itself was entirely remodelled and extended in the 1820s. Throughout the nineteenth century various additions continued to be made. In 1846, Daniel Robertson, the architect who had been planning the new garden at nearby Powerscourt, designed a stone balustrade for the terrace on the east front. In 1852, a new domed conservatory by the Scottish architect William Burn was added to the west front. The pattern of its pierced roof parapet was based on the tiara Lady Meath sold in order to pay for the conservatory. A floral parterre was laid out around a fountain as a setting for the conservatory, which crowned one axis of the parterre. At the end of the cross-axis an ornamental dairy was built, on the design of Sir George Hodson, an amateur architect, who also worked at neighboring Powerscourt.

Soon after these features were added at Killruddery, a hurricane blew down many of the trees in the old French-style garden and an extensive restoration had to take place. New statuary was purchased for it, probably at the great International Trade Fairs that took place in London and Dublin in the 1860s, for much of the statuary in the garden is signed by Kahl of Potsdam in Germany and Barbezat et Cie of Seine-et-Oise in France, both exhibitors at these fairs. As a result of these purchases, Killruddery has a fine collection of Victorian garden statuary.

So the garden remained until the present earl and countess of Meath came to

live at Killruddery after the Second World War and began to adapt its enormous house and garden to modern times. They reduced the size of the house in the 1950s and also set about reducing the maintenance requirements of the garden. The flower parterre was planted with yellow lily-flowered tulips for spring and pink roses and blue lavender for summer. Lady Meath made paved gardens around the base of the house, planting them with herbs and dwarf flowering shrubs to soften the stone. The joints of the paving are thick with the flowers of the pink-and-white daisy *Erigeron mucronatus* for most of the summer. Despite all this, Lord Meath frequently spent his entire weekends cutting his many acres of lawn.

Now Lord and Lady Meath have handed over Killruddery to their son and daughter-in-law, Lord and Lady Ardee. They work hard to maintain and, where possible, to restore their property. They have reroofed the conservatory in Plexiglas, tackled the cutting of the high hedges in the Beech Circle, and renewed the shrub borders. Under their energetic direction, the conservatory has become the venue for charity garden parties, plant sales, and musical events. At times like these the garden fills with the sound of the laughter and song of the elegantly dressed crowds for whom, after all, the French garden was invented.

The Gardens of Ireland

# Mount Usher

• • • • • • • • • • • • • • • • • • • • • • •

COUNTY WICKLOW
Mrs. Madeleine Jay

"The garden is quite unlike any other garden that I have ever seen, and to see it in the time of Lilies, Paeonies, Poppies and Delphiniums is to see much lovely colour amongst the rich greenery of the rising woodlands. In Autumn the colour is less brilliant but equally satisfying as the eye wanders from the Torch Lilies and Gladioli to the Blue Agapanthus, and thence to the Pine and Fir clad hills.

"Mount Usher is a charming example of the gardens that might be made in river valleys, especially those amongst the mountains and the hills. In such places there is often delightful shelter from violent winds, while the picturesque effects of the mountains and the hills offer charming prospects from the garden."

*The female catkins—sometimes up to ten inches long—of the Japanese poplar,* Populus maximowiczii, *which ripens its fruit in July.*

*Preceding pages:*
*The eucalyptus collection was begun in 1905 with an importation of seed from Sydney, Australia. This ribbon gum is one of the largest in Britain or Ireland.*

*Long vistas reach out from the house to opposite ends of the garden. The Palm Walk is lined with the Chusan palm,* Trachycarpus fortunei. *On either side is one of those meadows of bulbs and wildflowers in long grass recommended by William Robinson.*

So wrote William Robinson in *The English Flower Garden* (1883). In his earlier book, *The Wild Garden* (1870), he had criticized the influence of architects and architectural styles on garden design and affirmed that Nature itself should be the only true model for garden design. Effects in the garden should be modeled on those in the natural landscape, not determined by the architectural style of the house. A lawn should be like an ornamental meadow, a group of trees like a natural woodland, a pool like a natural pond. Plants should not be seen simply as colorful objects with which to decorate an architectural plan but should be appreciated for their own sake—their form and habit of growth, their seasonal changes and preferred habitat. Each garden should have as rich a variety of plantings as possible, so that its owners might learn about Nature in all her aspects.

This was a revolutionary approach at that time, but it was quickly adopted by two brothers, George and Edward Walpole, who were then eagerly developing the garden of their weekend house at Mount Usher, County Wicklow. The house and its one-acre garden had been bought in 1868 by their father who, realizing their great interest in its development, gave it to them in 1875. They were passionate plant collectors. Recognizing their enthusiasm and also the suitability of their garden for growing tender or subtropical plants, the director of the Botanic Gardens in Dublin, Sir Frederick Moore, kept the Walpoles supplied with plants and lists of plants they might purchase. Indeed, the Walpoles ransacked the nurseries of Europe for plants and imported some from Australia and Japan. Their growing collections forced them to acquire more and more of the neighboring land, the present acreage of twenty-two being built up over a period of sixty years. Had it not been for the Walpole brothers' discovery of William Robinson, Mount Usher might well have become simply a collectors' garden instead of the superb example of Robinsonian gardening it is today.

Robinson held that every garden should have a natural rather than an architectural focus. So at Mount Usher the house is to one side rather than at the center of the garden, and the river forms the natural focus of the design. The Walpoles began to develop the river's natural attractions by damming it at selected points so that the sound of falling water would fill the garden, and to create pools to reflect the plants along its banks and rocky shallows in which to grow marginal plants. Architectural features, where they were necessary, were treated minimally. For example, bridges crossing the river were designed on the suspension principle so they would look as light as possible.

Robinson had noticed that the marginal areas in nature—between woodland and meadow, or between water and dry ground, for example—always possessed the richest variety of plants, and he held that similar margins in gardens should be richly and thickly planted. So the Walpoles developed the banks of the river, and the many streams that feed it, as luxuriant features of their garden. In the shallows, ribbons of American and Chinese skunk cabbages have been naturalized; sheets of primula and mimulus spread in the mud between the boulders when the water level subsides in spring, and winter aconites flower in solid clumps on the banks. The foliage of huge-leaved gunnera and peltiphyllum glistens after rain. Groups of pampas grass, palms, bamboo, and flax are permanently reflected in the stiller reaches. The colors of azaleas, guelder roses, and hydrangeas in flower, and of maples in autumn, are reflected more fleetingly, according to season. The retaining walls by the house are curtained with the pink-and-white daisy *Erigeron mucronatus* throughout the summer. Dipping into the water nearby are the four enormous spreading or weeping conifers of which Mount Usher is especially proud, the

weeping hemlock, *Tsuga canadensis* 'Pendula', the spreading golden yew, *Taxus baccata* 'Dovastonii Aurea', and the striking Lawson cypresses, *Chamecyparis lawsoniana* 'Intertexta Pendula' and [*Chamaecyparis lawsoniana*] 'Tabuliformis'. Normally recommended for the small garden, here they have large size and spread.

The banks of the streams (some of them old mill races) that feed the river are also gardened in a Robinsonian way. The banks of one stream have been built up with stones to make a linear rock garden. The banks of another, which passes through a grove of trees, have been made into a ferncry with tender woodwardias and hymenophyllums. A third stream is edged with hostas and thick ribbons of candelabra primulas, polyanthus, and other primroses, and winds its way into a lily pond margined with ornamental rushes and water irises. Mount Usher, therefore, provides examples of many different forms of the wild water garden.

Natural woodlands have a different range of plants from those by watersides. Shrubby and herbaceous layers grow under the trees' canopy. Climbers scale the tree trunks in search of light, and bulbs flower fleetingly before the trees put on their leaves each spring. Robinson held that a grove of trees, no matter how small, would give gardeners an opportunity to grow the many wonderful bulbous plants from all over the world. At Mount Usher, rhododendrons and camellias are massed under the trees in considerable numbers. Huge-leaved *Rhododendron sinogrande* and *R. falconeri* are mixed with huge-flowered *R. x* 'Loderi'. Winter-flowering *R.*

*Robinson held that every garden should have a natural rather than an architectural focus. So it is at Mount Usher, where the river rather than the house is the focus of the garden.*

*The bark of the ribbon gum,* Eucalyptus viminalis, *is shed in long ribbons and is yellowish or white when first exposed.*

*Opposite page:*
*Bright orange deciduous azalea hybrids grow so tall they reach into the branches of palm trees.*

*barbatum* is close to summer-flowering *R.* 'Polar Bear'. Trilliums, lily-of-the-valley, and Solomon's seal carpet the ground between the native ferns. Western hemlock, Tasmanian blue gum, Kashmir cypress, Asiatic magnolias, and the Chinese *Picea likiangensis*, now huge trees, were planted in sheltered clearings among the oak. Here, shade is a welcome contrast to the sunlight of the water garden, and bird song fills the ear as the sound of falling water recedes. Such contrasts are the stuff of which good wild gardens are made.

A natural meadow contains wildflowers and bulbs growing through the grasses. It was Robinson's idea that lawns should approximate to this. At Mount Usher a broad meadow sweeps in front of the house and off in different directions into three grassy rides, each of which leads to a boundary of the property. Though each ride is flanked by layer upon layer of exotic plants, each also has a theme given by the repetition of one plant and from which it derives its name—the Palm, the Maple, or the Azalea Avenue. These provide welcome perspectives and long-distance focus in a garden otherwise so densely planted.

In February each year, the grass under the trees in the meadow becomes white with sheets of snowdrops and wood anemones, which are followed by patches of purple, white, and yellow crocus. Later the banks become blue with scillas and grape hyacinths, narcissi, and snake's head fritillaries. The bright colors of big drifts of daffodils and snowflakes are followed by the subtle colors of wildflowers and meadow grasses in patches where the grass has been left unmown. In autumn, darkly colored patches of autumn crocus (colchicum) and cyclamen emerge to finish the season of this meadow garden.

While building up these differing areas of Robinsonian wild garden, the Walpoles were also building up an important collections of trees—for example, of eucalyptus, southern beech (*Nothofagus*), and eucryphia. The eucalyptus group, comprising over seventy species, was begun in 1905 with seed imported from Australia. It was replenished when Robert Walpole imported a further consignment of seed in the 1950s from Melbourne. The southern beech collection started in 1928 has eight different species, and the eucryphia collection is best known for eucryphia 'Mount Usher', the natural hybrid that occurred in the garden between two Chilean species. These collections are not arranged in botanical groups as they might be in a botanic garden, however. They are mixed in with other rare trees which by contrast show off their individual characteristics to best advantage. The white stems of the eucalyptus, for example, are contrasted with the dark foliage of hemlock and cedar behind. The eucryphias are interplanted with hydrangeas so their summer flowering is combined. The nothofagus are positioned with spring-flowering trees to show off their sombre but finely made foliage. This is what Robinson had proposed.

The garden at Mount Usher was formed by four generations of Walpoles: by Edward Sr. from 1868 to 1875, by Edward Jr. and George from 1875 to the First World War, by E. H. Walpole until 1946, and then by his son Robert for about thirty-five years. It was this continuity of planting in a consistent style that gave Mount Usher such outstanding character. Now it is owned by Mrs. Madeleine Jay, who together with the head gardener, John Anderson, continues to plant and maintain, clearing areas that have become overgrown and repairing damage caused not only by occasional frost or storms, but also, sadly, by visitors, a problem that should not be underestimated in a garden that is open to the public. In a country that has many Robinsonian gardens, Mount Usher is the most typical and among the best conserved.

# Powerscourt

· · · · · · · · · · · · · · · · · · ·

COUNTY WICKLOW
Mr. and Mrs. Ralph Slazenger

Powerscourt lies in a shallow amphitheater of mountains watered by the Dargle, one of Ireland's scenic rivers. In this magnificent setting, in the third quarter of the nineteenth century, the seventh viscount Powerscourt created a garden of noble terraces leading the eye across a pool and a wooded valley to the Wicklow Mountains on the horizon. With a terrace half a mile long, flights of steps forty feet wide, and a fountain jet one hundred feet high, his creation was monumental in scale.

The great house, which had been built between 1731 and 1740 for Richard Wingfield, later first viscount Powerscourt, was modelled on

*One of a pair of stone gods that flank the boat house on Juggy's pond. The Triton fountain can be seen in the distance.*

*Preceding pages:*
*The charred shell of the once magnificent house presides over the terrace, which the designer, Daniel Robertson, based on one at the Villa Butera in Sicily.*

*The waterfall in the deer park is the highest in Ireland.*

the Villa Pisani near Venice. The rough slope below the house was cut into grass banks and terraces leading down to a circular pond (known as Juggy's Pond). Some say Richard Castle, the architect of the house, was responsible for this layout, others that it was one George Dean, who advertised himself in a Dublin newspaper in 1746 as having been "lately Gardener to Lord Viscount Powerscourt" and a designer of pleasure gardens and parterres. No sooner had these grand terraces been constructed than the formal terraced gardens went out of fashion. Already in 1752, the voguish Bishop Pococke derided the terraces at Powerscourt as being "too steep and unnatural." Yet Powerscourt had much to offer those who had embraced the new taste for the natural in the garden and landscape. The river Dargle flows below the house, with a magnificent waterfall, the largest in Ireland; the river valley and its surrounding mountains were a mecca for sophisticated tourists, and Lord Powerscourt generously built teahouses for their reception.

By 1841, another cycle of taste had brought the formal garden back into fashion again. Then Richard, the sixth viscount, great-great-grandson of the builder of the house, commissioned Daniel Robertson, a talented but dissolute architect, to make a new formal garden based on the old. Robertson had had to leave his native England under a cloud. In Ireland, he was soon under another. Mervyn, the seventh viscount, wrote of him:

"At the time he was drawing these plans . . . he was always in debt, and the

Sheriff's officers were after him. Warning being given of their approach to arrest him, he used to hide in the domes on the roof of the house. He was much given to drink and was never able to design or draw so well as when his brain was excited by sherry. He suffered from gout and used to be wheeled out on the terrace in a wheelbarrow, with a bottle of sherry, and so long as that lasted he was able to design and direct the workmen but when the sherry was finished he collapsed and was incapable of working till the drunken fit evaporated."

His design for the upper terrace, which he based on the Villa Butera in Sicily, was the only one completed. His patron, having gone to Italy to buy statuary for the garden, died in 1844 on his way home through France.

The statuary remained in packing cases for fourteen years until the heir, Mervyn, came of age, when he continued the project. With the help of a Scottish gardener, Alexander Robertson (no relation to Daniel), he began making the lower amphitheater of grass terraces we see today, employing about one hundred men with horses and carts to move the soil. Unfortunately, in 1860, in the midst of this difficult operation, Alexander Robertson died. Powerscourt wrote:

"He was at work at the semi-circular terraces on the Lower part near Juggy's Pond, and had just completed the east side of these, when he got an anthrax in his neck, which was cut (he was a very full-blooded man) and the exhaustion caused by the issue pulled him down so much that he died. His grave is in the old church-

*Above and overleaf:*
*A pair of* pegasi *are painted to look like bronze although they are made of zinc. They have a place of honor in the garden as they are taken from the Powerscourt coat of arms.*

*The Gardens of Ireland*

*Powerscourt*

yard at the east end of the terrace, near where his work is ended."

Undeterred, Powerscourt finished off the terraces at the lower end of the garden but was unsure how to deal with the middle. He traveled widely in Europe, visiting the gardens of Versailles, Schönbrunn near Vienna, and Schwetzingen near Mannheim, Germany, but was still without inspiration. So he consulted a series of professional landscape gardeners. The first was James Howe, who gave him a plan for scrollwork beds in 1865. But Howe died soon afterwards in circumstances that recall the activities of Daniel Robertson a generation earlier. The viscount wrote:

"Mr. Howe died shortly after this plan was completed, of drink. He had been at Glaslough, Co. Monagahan, laying out improvements for Col. Charles Lesley and was taken with *delirium tremens* and left, and only got home . . . in time to die there."

In the following year Lord Powerscourt consulted the more sober Mr. Broderick Thomas from London, without significant result, and then his neighbor, Sir George Hodson, an amateur architect, who suggested an ornamental platform, or perron, as a focal point at the center of the garden. This suggestion was adopted, and the result we see today. Formal plans were drawn up by Sir Francis Penrose, at that time architect to Saint Paul's Cathedral, London, to incorporate many of the architectural and sculptural features brought back by Lord Powerscourt from his travels in Europe. The platform floor was laid in a pattern of pebbles, the steps

*The Gardens of Ireland*

flanked by urns copied from some at Versailles, and the edge protected by a wrought-iron rail purchased from a castle in Germany, near Hesse. The lower side was designed as a wall fountain, with a splendid pair of figures representing Aeolus, the god of the winds. These had originally been in the garden of the duke of Arese in Italy but Prince Jerome Napoleon, nephew of the Emperor Napoleon III, had bought them for his own garden in Paris. There, water was made to gush from under their arms, and their mouths were connected to a gas main so that, on occasion, they might appear to breathe fire! They were rescued when the prince's palace was burned by the *communards* after the Franco-Prussian War and Lord Powerscourt bought them.

The garden had become, by now, an outdoor museum of sculpture. Winged figures of Fame and Victory for the top terrace, and winged horses or *pegasi* (the heraldic supporters of the family coat of arms), for the pool had been commissioned from Professor Hagan in Berlin. A design for the fountain in the pond, based on Bernini's fountain in the Piazza Barberini, was commissioned from Lawrence Macdonald, a sculptor then working in Rome. Macdonald also designed the heroic groups of Hector and Andromache, now standing on the upper terrace, and of Ajax with the body of Patroclus, at the end of the Monkey Puzzle Avenue. Powerscourt bought or commissioned something for the garden wherever he went. His visit to Paris in 1867 resulted in his purchase of the spectacular Golden Gates

*The English architect Sir Francis Penrose designed the paving of black and white pebbles gathered on the nearby beach at Bray.*

*Opposite page:*
*The upper terrace constructed between 1841 and 1843 is punctuated by alternating stone figures and vases. On the left is a winged figure of Fame commissioned in 1866 from Professor Hagen of Berlin; on the right is a copy of the Apollo Belvedere brought from Italy by the sixth viscount.*

*The Perspective Gate, painted in black and gold, was originally part of a screen in Bamberg cathedral in Germany.*

A vase of Carrara marble and a Portugal laurel clipped into a dome shape to resemble the clipped orange trees of Italian gardens decorate the upper terrace.

Opposite page:
The formal sunk garden designed by Edward Milner, Sir Joseph Paxton's assistant. A line of trees, each planted to commemorate the visit of an important personage to the garden, breaks the skyline above the terrace beyond.

A copy of the famous Laocoön in the Vatican Museum.

now forming one entrance to the demesne. In Naples in 1885, he bought bronze copies of the *Seated Mercury* and the *Sleeping Faun* excavated at nearby Herculaneum. He bought a pair of sarcophagi in a monastery garden in Rome and a pair of idols in a temple in Mysore. The "Venetian Gate," in the walled part of the garden was made in Venice in 1770. At other entrances he erected what are known as the Chorus Gate (an old German one) and the Perspective Gate, which has a trompe l'oeil design at its center and came originally from Bamberg Cathedral.

Lord Powerscourt's tree planting was on the same heroic scale as his travelling and collecting. At Powerscourt, the boundaries of the garden are not strictly defined, but rather they grade gently off into the neighboring woodland. In front, the trees have been planted to frame and enclose the garden yet open it to the view. His choice of so many tall conifers was no doubt inspired by the pointed peak of the Sugar Loaf Mountain behind. Lord Powerscourt specialized in the conifers of northwest America. A coast redwood (*Sequoia sempervirens*) from California, which he planted in 1866, is now the finest in Ireland. There is an unequalled Monterey cypress (*Cupressus macrocarpa*), 118 feet high with a multiple bole 15 feet across. Huge Sitka spruce (*Picea sitchensis*) and Douglas fir (*Pseudotsuga menziesii*) flourish in great numbers in the valley, as well as large stands of Caucasian fir (*Abies nordmanniana*) planted in 1867. In addition to the famous avenue of monkey puzzles (*Araucaria araucana*), there is a stand of one hundred of them

planted by Lord Powerscourt with his own hand in 1870. He also commenced the afforestation of the surrounding mountains. In the ten years between 1870 and 1880 he planted four hundred thousand trees annually. The figures speak for themselves. "Nobody," he wrote, "can say that I have not left my mark on the country."

The viscount's son, also Mervyn, lived at Powerscourt until his death in 1947. His gardening activities included laying out a small but hardly authentic Japanese garden and erecting a mock-mediaeval tower in the woods. So the garden remained, next cared for by Mervyn, the ninth viscount, and, after its sale in 1961, by Mr. and Mrs. Ralph Slazenger, its present owners.

An old garden needs to adapt or die. For over two hundred and fifty years, Powerscourt has been one of the great sights of Ireland. But the calamitous fire of 1974 gutted the house, and since then the garden has become the principal attraction. So this process of adaptation is taking place at Powerscourt, under the direction of the tourism manager, Miss Ailbhe Butler. July and August are the peak months for visitors, most of whom, of course, are the owners of small gardens. To satisfy their demand to see plants suitable for the small garden, a new double herbaceous border and a rose garden have been planted to one side of the main vista for which Powerscourt has so long been famous. Thus, a great aristocratic garden adapts to our democratic age.

The Gardens of Ireland

# Birr Castle

• • • • • • • • • • • • • • • •

## COUNTY OFFALY
### The Earl and Countess of Rosse

The gardens of Birr Castle are among the largest in Ireland. They cover 150 acres, including park, arboretum, and lake, but they are as notable for their fine design and the extreme rarity of many of the trees and shrubs as for their immense size. That such a garden—the result of over three centuries of planting in different periods and styles—should still constitute one harmonious whole is remarkable. No less remarkable is that Birr Castle is still gardened and cared for, out of its own resources, by the family that began its development so many centuries ago.

The castle, formerly the property of the Ely O'Carrolls, stands on a rocky precipice above the rushing waters of the river Camcor next to

*One of the bridges designed by the dowager Lady Rosse and made in the sawmill on the estate.*

*Preceding pages:*
*High hornbeam hedges trained overhead into a pattern of baroque vaulting surround the main formal garden.*

*Although parts of the castle date from about 1620, the facade facing the park was not constructed until the early nineteenth century, to the designs of the Irish architect John Johnston.*

the town of Birr. It was acquired by the Parsons family in 1620 and has been their home, with interruptions in the seventeenth century, for more than 350 years. Such continuity is unusual for Ireland because most noble families vacated their uncomfortable castles in the towns in favor of new Georgian houses in the country during the eighteenth century. Sir Laurence Parsons, later second earl of Rosse, simply turned his castle around, so that instead of facing the town it faced the landscape park that his father had made at the back. This park, with its classic serpentine lake, its broad, sloping lawns, and its clumps of huge beech trees, remains the setting and context of the garden today. Sir Laurence, disenchanted with Irish politics, concentrated on developing his estate. With the help of his architect, John Johnston, he built a new, twin-towered entrance gateway and a church on axis with it, giving his castle a more architectural aspect. An elegant iron suspension bridge crossing the river Camcor also dates from this period; in its advanced technology it seems to anticipate the achievements of the family in the next generations.

Sir Laurence's son, William, the third earl, an astronomer and president of the Royal Society, was married to Mary Field, a Yorkshire heiress who shared his scientific and technical interests. On succeeding to the title in 1841, he commenced the construction of the giant telescope in the park in front of the castle. Known as "The Leviathan of Parsonstown" (Birr was then known as Parsonstown), it was until 1917 the largest reflecting telescope in the world. (Its tube, over fifty feet long and seven feet wide, can be seen today.) Sir William must have felt the instrument would look peculiar in an ornamental park, so he dressed up its supporting walls with Gothic arcading and battlements to make it look like a folly. Lady Rosse, an energetic and enterprising woman and a pioneer photographer, had ornamental earth ramparts built around the castle to the designs of her uncle, Colonel Richard Wharton Myddleton. The project was undertaken during the Famine years as a means of providing relief. To span the ramparts, a new gatehouse was constructed, the iron gates being cast in the workshop set up for the telescope's construction. A fernery and a collection of conifers completed the Earl and Countess's contribution to the park at Birr. This rich and varied history of construction and planting is important in understanding the setting in which the gardens were made and in which we see them today.

It was William, the fifth earl, who, in 1912, made the first major contribution to Birr as a place of outstanding botanical and horticultural interest. He purchased a collection of plants at the closing-down sale of the English nursery firm of Sir James Veitch. These are the cornerstone of the gardens today. Among them were plants grown from seed collected by the English plant hunter E. H. Wilson in the Himalayas. The *Magnolia delavayi* below the castle was raised from seed collected by Wilson in western China in 1900 and so is among the first grown in the Western world. It is now more than twenty feet high and survives the frosts at Birr because it is sheltered by one of Colonel Myddleton's rampart walls. The *Carrierea calycina* by the river was discovered by Wilson in western China in 1908 and considered by him, because of the beauty of its flower, to be a great acquisition. Unfortunately it has not lived up to its promise, having died in most gardens to which it was introduced. The one at Birr is the best remaining. Not all of Wilson's introductions at Birr have been so successful, however. Many of his conifers have died off before reaching maturity. But some failures are inevitable in the exciting process of pioneering new plants for our gardens, and, indeed, there is often as much to be learned from the failures as from the successes.

*The Gardens of Ireland*

Carrying on the tradition established by the fifth earl at the beginning of the century, one of the overriding interests of successive earls of Rosse since then has been the introduction of new plants to Birr, not from nurseries or other gardens of the west, but directly from the wild, and in particular from the Orient. Birr, being in an inland county, has a lower rainfall and sharper frosts than gardens in the maritime counties. So subtropical plants from the southern hemisphere of the world, which are so characteristic of most Irish gardens, cannot be grown here. Nor, because of the alkaline soil, can that other great group of plants so characteristic of Irish gardens, the rhododendrons and camellias, be grown successfully. These severe restrictions have led to a concentration on plants originating in the Far East, and in particular in the Himalayas.

When the sixth earl inherited Birr in 1918 at the age of eleven, he inherited not so much a garden as the beginnings of a collection of rare Asian plants set in an ancestral landscape park. When he was old enough, he built upon his father's initiative, planting additional trees and shrubs from the Far East. Lord Headfort, whose garden in County Meath had a remarkable collection of Wilson-introduced plants, encouraged him with many gifts. Lord Rosse subscribed to the plant-hunting expeditions into the Himalayas of Frank Kingdon Ward, raising many new plants from the seed he obtained. In 1938, he was given a copy of the seed catalogue of Lushan Botanical Garden in northern China, and the seed he ordered from it

*Large-leaved gunnera by the rushing river Camcor provides a foreground to the castle and its terrace wall.*

*Close-ups at Birr: This viola originated in the garden of William Robinson at Gravetye. Magnolias are a special feature here. Spring bedding with forget-me-nots and tulips gives concentrated color.*

have resulted in some of the rarest trees in the garden. Of two limes, for example, *Tilia henryana* is known to be growing in only one other location outside China (Les Barres, in France), and *Tilia chingiana* is not grown anywhere outside its native land. Birr was becoming a reservoir for some of the rarest trees and shrubs in cultivation in the world.

In 1935, Lord Rosse had married Anne, daughter of Lieutenant Colonel L. C. R. Messel, whose garden at Nymans in Hampshire, England, was, and still is, one of the finest in the world. (It is now administered by the National Trust.) His wife's background, therefore, enabled her to share to the utmost her husband's interest.

On their honeymoon in Peking, they collected cones of Chinese arborvitae (*Thuja orientalis*) in the courtyard of the Temple of Confucius, and of Chinese pine (*Pinus tabuliformis*) in the Forbidden City. Maturing trees grown from these cones now grace the park at Birr. While in Peking, they met Professor Hu, a Chinese botanist who fired them with enthusiasm for the many colorful plants that still awaited discovery in the Chinese interior. On their return, Lord Rosse galvanized a group of like-minded enthusiasts to sponsor a series of plant-hunting expeditions into the Chinese interior between 1937 and 1940. Unfortunately the outbreak of war prevented the seed from all but the first expedition from ever reaching Europe.

Many and rare plants from this expedition are now growing at Birr. One, a tree peony, *Paeonia delavayi*, pollinated a neighboring tree peony, *Paeonia lutea ludlowii*, collected by the hunters Ludlow and Sheriff in China's Tsangpo Gorge in 1926, to give a new, award-winning hybrid; it has been appropriately named *Paeonia* 'Anne Rosse'. Another rare tree collected by the Hu expedition is *Koelreuteria bipinnata*, an unusual member of the golden-rain tree family that can be seen in only one other garden in Europe, La Mortola in Italy.

Although Birr was becoming a mecca for lovers of rare trees, the new and beautiful design of the garden was beginning also to reflect the interest of Lord and Lady Rosse in the arts. Indeed, Lady Rosse (now the dowager countess of Rosse) is a member of an artistically gifted family: her late brother, Oliver Messel, was a well-known theatrical and interior designer, and her son, the earl of Snowdon, is a remarkable photographer.

In celebration of their marriage, Lord and Lady Rosse created a box parterre in a corner of the old walled kitchen garden. The centerpiece of the pattern was a pair of intertwined *R*s. The idea derived from a seventeenth-century Bavarian design they discovered in a book in Colonel Messel's library. Stone urns in an appropriate rococo style were obtained for the center path and hornbeams planted in alleys around the outside of the garden. These are now most distinctive because they were planted farther apart than normal. Instead of making the usual green tunnel, they have formed a light, ribbed structure with ribbons of snowdrops along the base in winter. It was originally intended that the trees would be trained to form a flat ceiling overhead. However, the forced neglect of the war years resulted in the overhead branches developing gentle curves. Lord and Lady Rosse seized the opportunity to develop these curves further and so created the baroque hornbeam vault we see in the garden today. Twin figures of the Graces, embowered in roses, terminate these walks, and a seat designed by Lady Rosse in a fanciful baroque style presides at one end. Shrub roses, lilac hybrids, delphiniums, irises, and many other flowers were planted to wrap this fine design with rich color.

A suite of formal gardens make the whole area an essay in the modern compartmented style of gardening. The owner of the small garden will find much to inspire

*A fanciful seat in the baroque style designed by the dowager countess of Rosse and made by the carpenter on the estate.*

*The late Lord Rosse hybridized the yellow tree peony* Paeonia lutea ludlowii *with the red* P. delavayi *to create this new tree peony, which he named 'Anne Rosse'.*

him in each of these garden "rooms." One has a circular colonnade with mauve wisteria clambering on it and peonies and pinks at its feet. Another has silver-leaved pears contrasting with dark yew hedges behind. The lower terrace is devoted to masses of old and rugosa roses. A walk is lined with giant box trees, three centuries old and thirty-five feet high. They have been pruned except at the top to form a green cathedral vault. Another walk is focused on the Edwardian greenhouse supplied by Richardson and which has just been restored.

Another design project inaugurated by the earl and countess of Rosse was the creation of a flower garden near the castle. First, they had to remove part of Colonel Myddleton's rampart walls—no easy task of earthmoving—so they could develop a series of terraces leading down from the castle to the river below. The conventional terrace garden is rectangular, but here the Rosses used the angles of the castle walls and the ramparts to develop a trapezoidal rather than a rectangular design, a design reminiscent of the angular harmonies of Braque or Picasso paintings of that period. Vibrant reds and yellows dominate the wide, angular borders, cleverly arranged so that from some points of view the castle walls appear to rise straight out of the herbaceous plantings. Around them is a flurry of incident: climbers expertly and picturesquely tied up to the castle walls, a secret rose garden, the ancient well of Saint Brendan, and, nearby, broad groups of trees and shrubs selected for autumn color.

Steps lead down to a river bank where the Rosses developed a wild river garden in the Robinsonian tradition, of which examples already existed in Ireland, as at Mount Usher and Annes Grove. As always at Birr, the trees predominate, the tallest being a gray poplar (*Populus canescens*), at 110 feet among the tallest in these islands. Huge yews, a Monterey cypress (*Cupressus macrocarpa*) 100 feet tall, and a Himalayan juniper (*Juniperus recurva*) with a spread of 40 feet are among the conifers that provide a series of massive backcloths for the flowering of the proportionally immense magnolias in spring. The time scale for flowering is equally heroic. Of three tree magnolias planted in 1946, *M. dawsoniana* flowered first in 1961, *M. campbellii mollicomata* bloomed for the first time in 1962, and *M. campbellii* has waited until recently. It is only a gardener with patience and confidence in the future who will plant magnolias so slow to bloom. Once blooming, however, these trees reward his patience with some of the most spectacular blossoms a garden can offer. The tallest of the magnolias is *M. x veitchii*; though planted only in 1934, it is reaching the proportions of a forest tree. Of special interest are the "family" magnolias, new hybrids that have been registered under the names 'Leonard Messel' (the Dowager Lady Rosse's father), 'Anne Rosse', and 'Michael Rosse' (her late husband).

Silhouetted against the dark conifers are Japanese maples in various tints of red, purple, and yellow-green. There are over fifty species as well as numerous varieties located throughout the park, helping to fire it with flaming color during the fall.

It is a surprise to see so many magnolias and maples flourishing on this alkaline soil. They are generally held to prefer acid soil, on which they are often seen associated with an underlayer of acid-loving shrubs such as rhododendrons and camellias (as can be seen at another great garden, Mount Congreve). At Birr, however, they are seen in unusual association with lime-loving shrubs such as philadelphus, deutzias, and lilacs, and the evergreen barberries, mahonias, viburnums, and cotoneasters. This makes for a paler, lighter color scheme. Under the shrubs and trees are flowing patches of the ground-covering blue-eyed Mary (*Omphalodes cappadocica*), pulmonarias (in the red-, pink-, and white-flowering varieties), and periwinkles. Ferns, bergenias, epimediums, and brightly variegated ivies are used to carpet large shaded areas. The swirling patterns of ground cover give generous movement to the design. As in every part of the garden, there are specimens of interest to the dendrologist. Here is an *Ehretia dicksonii*, a rare flowering tree first introduced by Wilson from China.

Through the river garden, one reaches the head of the lake, its broad, still reaches contrasting with the rush of the river in the garden we have just left. A pair of bronze cranes and a half-submerged boathouse tinge this still backwater with romantic melancholy. Here in the lagoon garden, swans drift silently among the bullrushes. Spring brings the blossom of American dogwoods and the Japanese snowball viburnum (*Viburnum plicatum tomentosum*) along the banks and autumn the vivid coloring of maples and Sargent cherry. From here the view opens up into a wide arc of water and sky, with golden and cricket-bat willows, weeping beeches, and one of the three original specimens of the dawn redwood (*Metasequoia glyptostroboides*) brought to England, sent to Birr for trial from Kew Gardens. All is serenity and peace.

One can look back across the lake and park to the castle in the distance. The grass floor of the park was planted by the Rosses with hundreds of thousands of daffodils, each great group of a single variety. They often cluster around huge trees

*Birr Castle*

An avenue of giant box trees, over thirty-four feet tall, presides over a formal garden bedded out with silver lamb's ears and the purple-leaved dahlia 'Bishop of Llandaff'.

Opposite page:
The tall column of an unusual, fastigiate tulip tree, Liriodendron tulipifera 'Fastigiatum', and a gray poplar, Populus canescens, at 110 feet the tallest tree at Birr, stand side by side in the river garden.

and lighten their shadows in spring. Threaded among the larger trees are groups of small flowering trees (mainly of the Rosaceae family—flowering cherries, crab apples, cotoneasters, and photinias—in which the late Lord Rosse specialized). They lighten the park with their blossom in spring, fire it with color in the autumn, and berry it brightly in winter.

The importance of a garden like Birr today lies not only in its large-scale aesthetic effects, spectacular though these are, but also in the important contribution to the sciences of botany and horticulture it continues to make. This can be illustrated by the five trees of Chinese or tea crab apple (*Malus hupehensis*) in the garden. One was raised from seed collected in China by Wilson; another, of unknown origin, was received from the botanic garden at Glasnevin, Dublin; and the last three were raised from seed collected in its native land by George Forrest in 1904. Though they are all crab apples and flower at the same time, that is about as far as the similarity goes. Here is food for thought and research by the botanist.

Botanical conservation, a special interest of the present earl, is also served through the active conservation of the arboretum at Birr. Considerable effort goes into the identification of the trees in the collection, their classification in order of botanical importance, and the development of a selective system of maintenance based on this classification. Exceptional measures are sometimes required to preserve rare species in the collection. For example, many of the Chinese conifers have failed or been blown down. To preserve the species in the collection, grafts are made and young plants produced from them. (It is significant that one of the gardening staff at Birr holds the title and post of head propagator—most exceptional for a privately owned garden.) As the wholesale destruction of trees in their native habitats continues throughout the world, rare collections like that at Birr may become important sources of part of the world's vegetation in the future. Therein lies their incalculable importance.

The sixth earl died in 1979 and Birr is now in the charge of his son, who has given new vigor to its conservation. Not only is he continuing to enrich the plant collections by subscribing to the plant-hunting expeditions in China of Roy Lancaster (himself joining an expedition of the International Dendrology Society to Nepal in 1984), but he sees Birr in a new light—as the vast store of artistic and scientific heritage that it is. It is an educational resource that we in Ireland ignore at our peril. Among the measures Lord Rosse has taken to ensure its future is the establishment of the Birr Scientific Heritage Foundation.

A garden that is the result of three centuries of continuous planting integrated into one harmonious whole is an increasing rarity in the world today. The garden of Birr Castle, where art and science are happily conjoined, is a precious commodity which, if destroyed, could never be replaced.

*Birr Castle*

The Gardens of Ireland

# Slevyre

. . . . . . . . . . . . . . . . . . . .

**COUNTY TIPPERARY**
Brigadier and Mrs. W. S. Hickie

A lane leads off the road into an ash wood. Through the shadows, the drive continues and then, suddenly, emerges again into the light, the dappled light of an orchard. In front is the door of the pavilion-like house built by Brigadier and Mrs. Hickie about fifteen years ago. Into the shadows once more, this time of the house, and one emerges into the light again on the other side and to an unexpected view of the rising ground and a bell tower. The bell tower belongs to the Victorian mansion (now a convent) that the Hickies left to build their present house. This alternation of light and shade is one of the secrets of a good garden.

Each flagstone of the terrace is outlined with a band of lady's mantle, cut with a rotary mower during summer.

Preceding pages:
A wall planting of Senecio 'Sunshine', the orange-peel clematis, Clematis tangutica, and the climbing form of the rose 'Shot Silk'.

Apple trees provide the setting for the pavilionlike house designed by Brigadier and Mrs. Hickie in 1970.

With a house like Slevyre, fruit trees rather than forest trees give just the right scale. They grow rapidly, are gay in their flowering, and give useful promise of fruit. The grass beneath can be planted with snowdrops, crocus, or daffodils, which always look their best under the blossom of cherry, apple, or pear trees in spring. If planted thickly and formally, fruit trees can frame the house and establish a strong theme for the garden. There is one disadvantage—the trees may be dull between the blossom of spring and the fruit of autumn. The Hickies have solved this summer problem by interplanting in the grass between the trees large groups of shrub roses that are allowed to grow, with little pruning, into large, free-standing specimens. The rambler roses, like 'Albertine' and 'Felicite et Perpetue', the latter keeping its glossy, light green leaves through mild winters, need a loose framework of props and stakes to grow on. The rugosa rose 'Blanc Double de Coubert' has fine moss green foliage to add to the soft and sumptuous color of its flowers. Other roses, like *R. filipes*, which foams with white flowers in early summer, and the yellow *R.* 'Emily Gray', climb into apple trees.

The rose theme is taken up on the walls of the house. Here pink and apricot climbers such as 'Shot Silk', 'Madame Butterfly', and 'Agnes' warm and soften the gray color of the plaster and stone. Their thick ankles are hidden beneath a long, low, loose planting of silver and pale-foliaged shrubs—senecio, lavender, rosemary, and Jerusalem sage—which have been allowed room to sprawl over and enjoy the heat of the gravel. It is surprising that these shrubs, which like a light,

134                    *The Gardens of Ireland*

shallow soil, are planted so frequently with roses, which like a heavy, deep soil. On the other hand, they flower together and the silver foliage of the smaller shrubs sets off the brighter colors of the roses and the green of their foliage.

Glazed doors through the central part of the house enhance the effect of a garden pavilion. One emerges from the house onto a sunken flagstone terrace almost engulfed by the lady's mantle, *Alchemilla mollis*, that grows in every crack in the paving. It makes a thick luxuriant carpet and its rounded hoary leaves trap raindrops, which glisten on their surfaces for many hours after summer showers. From June to August it sends up sprays of flowers that give the effect of a lime-green haze in the summer's heat. The center part of the terrace is mown with a rotary mower and thus each paving flag is outlined by a thick band of alchemilla leaf, two inches high. It responds perfectly to this treatment.

A wide lawn slopes across the line of the terrace. It is unplanted in order to emphasize the fine fall of the ground and a group of large oak, ash, and sycamore trees, which make a prominent, sculptural focal point near the house. The fine texture of the mown lawn is contrasted with the long grass in the meadow beyond, for one meets the other without barrier. Each year the junction between the two is remade by Brigadier Hickie's lawn mower so that it sweeps and curves to underline the shape of the slope. The slope also cleverly conceals the massive bulk of the old house; only its high bell tower is visible, looking like a folly in a park. To one side the lawn rises to the skyline, against which there is a wide, informal planting of

*Above:*
Helichrysum splendidum, *a remarkably hardy gray-leaved shrub; the York and Lancaster rose; hoary leaves of lady's mantle.*

*Above, left:*
Senecio 'Sunshine' *spills over the entrance steps on either side.*

*In the kitchen garden, lady's mantle and yarrow are backed by the York and Lancaster rose, its streaked purplish-pink and white flowers recalling the War of the Roses.*

*The bell tower of the mansion the Hickies left behind to build their present house now looks like a folly in the park.*

*Opposite page:*
*Lough Derg, one of Ireland's largest lakes, is glimpsed in spring through the tall trunks of an old oak wood carpeted with bluebells.*

lilacs and roses. To the other, it descends to give a peep of the lake of Lough Derg. The surface of its water gleams through an opening in an old oak and bluebell wood; here again the leitmotif of Slevyre is exemplified.

The Hickies made their new kitchen garden in the traditional form of a walled enclosure at some distance from the house. Its walls on the outside are entirely clothed with the climbing hydrangea, *Hydrangea petiolaris*, winter jasmine, ceanothus, clipped forsythia, single *Kerria japonica*, and rambling roses such as 'Francis Lester'. Within, the scale of planting changes to compact groups of vegetables, soft fruits, and flowers for cutting. What gives it its particular charm is the presence of wildflowers, like the violas from the nearby mountains of Slieve Bloom, which are woven through the more orderly ranks of vegetable and flower produce. It is interesting that when the Hickies speak of "the garden," they refer to this kitchen garden. When referring to the rest of their grounds they retain traditional usage of the "park" or the "pleasure grounds."

Pictures or furniture from different periods make the interior of a house more interesting. Similarly, plants popular in different periods make a garden more interesting. A whiff of nostalgia is provided by huge shrubby honeysuckle, *Lonicera chrysantha*, often seen in Victorian gardens but seldom planted today.

Brigadier Hickie was for many years an active member of An Taisce, the Irish National Trust, and takes a keen interest in conservation. It is not surprising, therefore, that the Hickies try to encourage wildflowers in their garden. Particularly remarkable are the orchids and the colony of sweet woodruff on a bank at the edge of a piece of woodland. Slevyre is a garden of many characters welded into one harmonious, discreetly understated whole. It has been made with a fine feel for the landscape, a judicious choice of plants, and the purest of tastes.

*The Gardens of Ireland*

*Slevyre*

# Killineer

· · · · · · · · · · · · · · · · · · · · · · ·

COUNTY LOUTH
Miss Grace Carroll

Gardens made a hundred years ago are today too labor-intensive in planting and design to be maintained with ease. Manicured lawns that boast razor-sharp edges, gravel paths smoothly raked, and greenhouses in which plants are raised to fill the summer flower beds are little in evidence now. Yet there is one garden in Ireland, Killineer, where all these things can still be seen. Made soon after the house was built in 1836, it is still impeccably maintained by its owner, Miss Grace Carroll.

The white-stuccoed Regency house gleams in the sunlight above broad terraces leading down to a lake, the focal point of the garden.

*The clear light of early summer creates a pattern of light and shade across the lawn sloping from the house to the lake.*

*Preceding pages:*
*The dappled light of a woodland edge tempers the hot colors of deciduous azalea.*

*A wisteria-clad pergola, with golden St. John's wort and orange wallflowers at the base of its pillars, frames the portico of the house.*

Each terrace is linked to the next by steps and path until the path divides around a sloping lawn and then reunites by the lakeside. Balanced plantings grace each terrace. On the first is a wisteria-clad pergola with golden Saint John's Wort (hypericum) around the feet of its pillars and lines of urns on either side. In spring, they are filled with orange wallflowers, in summer with scarlet geraniums. On the second terrace is a pair of vases on pedestals of twining dolphins wrought in stone. Around the bases are beds of mauve ageratum fringed with silvery Senecio *cinerara* 'Candicans', making a striking contrast with the green of the grass. Behind grow clumps of pampas grass, their silky plumes silvery in the darkening autumn days. Common laurel (*Prunus laurocerasas*) clipped flat and like a tabletop, a feature known to our grandparents as a "laurel lawn," fills the lowest terrace. On the oval lawn before it stand beautifully grown and symmetrical specimens of Lawson cypress gently feathered to the ground. Among them are the golden *Chamecyparis lawsoniana* 'Lutea' and the bluish *Chamaecyparis lawsoniana* 'Triomphe de Boskoop'. *Sorbaria arborea*, with its elegant pinnate leaves and creamy panicles of flower, spreads itself luxuriantly on the lawn nearby, and that time-honored Victorian color clash of mauve ponticum rhododendron with yellow azalea is vivid beneath the trees. The paths are decorated with rose arches on which are trained rambling roses like 'Dorothy Perkins', with its clustered flowers in shocking pink, and 'American Pillar', with a white eye in its single pink bloom.

By the lake a choice of paths must be made. One leads into a woodland garden made by Miss Carroll's parents with the help of Leslie Slinger of the famous Slieve Donard Nursery in Northern Ireland. Intimately scaled grass paths wind in and out of lush plantings in the half-shade. Bamboo curves among the trees. Large clumps of daylilies, their rushy leaves an ideal complement for their trumpet flowers, weave among the coarser foliage of *Rodgersia pinnata*, which becomes bronze through the season. Sinuous drifts of pink primulas sow themselves along the edges of the paths, their flow sometimes interrupted by the luminous blue of a Himalayan poppy (*Meconopsis betonicifolia*). Giant-leaved gunneras loom over leathery-leaved bergenias and ornamental grasses grow around lace-cap hydrangeas. The dusky red of astilbe flowers contrasts with the steely blue of hosta leaves. This small garden is an object lesson in flower and foliage contrasts.

Emerging into the sunlight on the far bank of the lake, one can look back at the house, now reflected in the water, from a small paved garden "room" enclosed in escallonia hedges, which glisten after rain. Two seats take advantage of the scent of an old philadelphus. Tiny thymes and campanulas form hummocks on the paving around the lily tank at the center. Lavenders and spotted pulmonarias edge the beds of polyanthus and primroses, which are succeeded in summer by pink phloxes and creamy astilbes. An old cottage rose completes this softly colored planting scheme inspired by Gertrude Jekyll.

*The white-stuccoed house, built in 1836, presides over broad terraces and lawns that gradually give way to a wilder atmosphere as the garden merges with the countryside.*

A narrow neck of the lake is crossed by a
delicate wrought-iron bridge in the shade of a
flowering laburnum tree.

Opposite page:
Candelabra primula seedlings by the water's
edge and Sorbaria arborea, with its creamy
panicles of flowers, add color to the sober
greens of the Victorian garden.

Around the lakeside, light willows contrast with dark yews, the vertical spears
of iris with the flat pads of water lilies, until one reaches a narrow neck where the
water is crossed by a delicate wrought-iron bridge. Next to it, a garden temple is
reflected in the water. This arm of the lake is overhung in a wilder way by woodland trees; their shadows rest the eye.

Through the wood the kitchen garden is reached. It is one of the best stocked
and managed in Ireland. Apple, cherry, pear, and plum trees screen blocks of
succulent soft fruit and furrowed rows of vegetables. Sweet peas are strictly trained
on ranks of bamboo canes, and greenhouses teem with seed trays and pot plants.

In contrast to the strictly controlled fruit and vegetable cultures are the flower
borders, so full of plants that they threaten to engulf the paths that separate them.
Lady's mantle forms a virtual drugget under one's feet. Orange alstroemerias, white
sisyrinchiums, metallic blue globe thistles and dusty-yellow yarrows flower in the
borders, which slope from front to back. Turk's cap lilies are sweetly saccharine
with purple phlox. Sidalceas blooming with the fading flowers of solidago and
rambling roses flowering among the early berries of pyracantha are reminders of
approaching autumn.

Such perfection, of course, is not easily come by. Yet on a warm summer's
Sunday, when only the ducks disturb the peace and a swan glides smoothly on the
lake, one can almost hear the rustle of a lady's crinoline and the tap of her escort's
cane on the gravel in this superbly maintained Victorian garden.

*Killineer*

The Gardens of Ireland

# Butterstream

· · · · · · · · · · · · · · · · · ·

COUNTY MEATH
Mr. Jim Reynolds

Jim Reynolds's house is what is known in Ireland as a "gentleman's cottage." Although the building was designed to look like a cottage, it has a surprisingly large number of well-proportioned rooms inside. Between the cottage and the stream that gives the property its name, Mr. Reynolds has made a series of interlinked gardens on an appropriately cottage-garden scale. Vita Sackville-West, the creator of the garden at Sissinghurst Castle in Kent, once described the famous compartmented garden of Hidcote in Gloucestershire as "a cottage-garden on the most glorified scale." This can also describe the garden at Butterstream. Here too, a wild garden, a rose garden, a white garden, a pool garden, a

*The orange flower spikes of* Ligularia przewalski *'The Rocket' stand erect on black stems.*

*Preceding pages:*
*The gate, a typical example of Irish Victorian ironwork, leads into an enclosure of open lawn bounded by purple beech hedges, its simplicity of design in contrast to the intensive planting of the rest of the garden.*

*The wings of the "gentleman's cottage" shelter the sun-loving* Yucca gloriosa.

herbaceous garden, and others make up a series of small "rooms," or compartments, each private and secret, the whole only gradually unfolding as one walks around.

Butterstream is set in a flat country of fields, trees, and sky on the edge of the town of Trim, its hedged enclosures effectively shutting out any sight of the surrounding housing. As at Sissinghurst, there are no large exotic trees—only those that existed when the garden was made, which ensure the garden's blend with the surrounding countryside. Although at Sissinghurst and Hidcote each compartment is formally planned yet freely planted, at Butterstream some compartments are both planned and planted informally. Two in particular, the wild garden and the herbaceous garden, exhibit a more modern influence in their use, respectively, of ground cover and island herbaceous beds.

There are many advantages to a garden of "rooms." Each compartment can be planned to reach a climax in a different season. A rose garden can become an explosion of bloom in June and July with an intensity of color denied to an all-year-round planting. Endless experimentation and change can take place, for one compartment can be altered without seriously affecting the look of the garden as a whole. Such a garden, therefore, need never remain static. Whole groups of plants can be regularly moved to better places. Every season the garden can be reinvigorated with new varieties and fresh ideas. So it is the antithesis of the modern labor-saving garden of trees and shrubs planted in permanent positions and left to mature over many years. As Jim Reynolds reckons on spending thirty-five hours per week in his garden, it is truly a style for the enthusiast.

To give the old-fashioned, cottagey look that is a major element of this style, the gates, urns, pillars, and paving with which each compartment is furnished must be old—or at least made of old materials. Gardeners like Jim Reynolds are always on the lookout for stockpiles of old paving stones or weathered bricks that can be made into paths or steps, gates from old abandoned gardens that might serve to divide one garden room from another, doorways or porticos from houses about to be demolished that can be used as focal points or temple fronts. Being a professional archaeologist, Jim Reynolds has been in a position to acquire many splendid ornaments to decorate his garden.

Similarly, species or old plant varieties are preferred to modern hybrids in planting this kind of garden. With the use of secateurs, shears, and string kept to a minimum, plants are allowed to relax into a natural but profuse habit of growth. In a similar bid to provide a natural look, selective self-seeding of certain plants is encouraged among the borders and in the paving. For example, at Butterstream many varieties of miniature violas form rampant and colorful rugs of flower between the taller perennials.

A garden with mixed planting for some color at every season of the year can never achieve the brilliance of color at any one time that can be planned for a single room in a many-compartmented garden. The compartment can focus on one color only, as in the white garden at Butterstream, or on a group of colors, as in the foliage garden, with flowers of red, orange, or yellow. Or it may be devoted to one family of plants, as in the rose garden, or be given over to groups of plants, as in the herbaceous garden, or to a succession of plants, as in the wild garden. Or the compartment may focus simply on an architectural feature, as in the pool garden.

The white garden is enclosed by beech hedges and each of its beds is neatly edged with box. White delphiniums, campanulas, and agapanthus rise from a bed

*The Gardens of Ireland*

of the silver foliage of artemisia and stachys. From one of the beds climbing musk roses, such as *Rosa longicuspis, R. filipes,* and *R. 'Rambling Rector',* foam up the trunks of hornbeam trees to flower against the sky.

The foliage garden relies on the impact of different foliage variations. Flowering amid the grassy foliage of coppery-yellow daylilies are scarlet *Crocosmia masonorum* 'Lucifer'; orange-yellow *Ligularia dentata,* with leaves sometimes eighteen inches across; and *Ligularia przewalski* 'The Rocket', its orange flower spikes and much-divided leaves erect on almost black stems (which prompt the notion of a garden of only black-stemmed plants).

The rose garden within beech hedges offers a marvelous contrast between formal design and exuberant planting. A collection of musk, damask, Bourbon, and gallica roses, flowering mainly in colors from pink to crimson, are corseted with props and stakes and confined to their beds by trim box hedges, which also serve to hide their unsightly ankles.

The island beds and borders of the herbaceous garden are planted magnificently. The grouping of plants by height provides a vivid three-dimensional effect, and the repetition of certain groups of plants provides underlying unity of design. Tall groups of sea kale (*Crambe cordifolia*), goat's beard (*Aruncus dioicus*), and plume poppy (*Macleaya cordata*) link the back of the border to the trees behind. Low groups of salvias, campanulas, and violas link it to the grass in front. The

*The white garden is furnished with delphiniums, bellflowers, and astrantias—all in their white forms—and with the green-and-white striped ribbongrass,* Phalaris arundinacea picta, *and a statuesque clump of Scotch thistle in the rear.*

148          *The Gardens of Ireland*

centers of the beds glow with the colors of hundreds of plants, outstanding among them the tall, brightly colored bergamots and the even taller foxtail lilies, with their yellow and apricot spires, six to eight feet high, waving gently in the wind.

The wild garden is designed with a succession of ground-cover plants. The dying foliage of its spring carpet of polyanthus and other primulas is masked by the emergent foliage of a summer carpet of hostas. A pool garden is Jim Reynolds's latest creation. Its design has various antecedents—the Viridarium at Pompeii, Harold Peto's Italian garden at Ilnacullin, and Rosemary Verey's pool garden at Barnsley in Gloucestershire. Each has a temple designed to be reflected in a pool.

Because of the hospitality of the Irish climate, many Irish gardens are made in a natural style to accommodate large collections of unusual trees and shrubs. Butterstream is a welcome contrast, a garden of firm design yet profuse planting and one that specializes in nonwoody plants, which provide solid, concentrated color in a way that trees and shrubs can never do.

*The foliage garden enclosed by beech hedges.*

*Opposite page:*
*The plants in the perennial borders are grouped by height to give a vivid three-dimensional effect, with certain groups repeated to give unity to the design. The spikes of foxtail lilies such as the yellow* Eremurus bungei *provide punctuation points. Here they thrive on a heavy clay soil, although a light soil is recommended for them. To the left is a dark form of* Salvia x superba *and to the right the comfrey* Symphytum x uplandicum *'Variegata', with large variegated leaves.*

*The Gardens of Ireland*

# Beaulieu

• • • • • • • • • • • • • • • • • • •

## COUNTY LOUTH
### Mr. and Mrs. Nesbit Waddington

As an estate, Beaulieu has existed for nearly eight hundred years. The present house, of stone with red brick facings, was built over three hundred years ago, and Mrs. Nesbit Waddington is the eighth-generation descendant of its builder, William Tichborne.

The Dutch-inspired house, which is approached by a short avenue of limes, looks out over formal grass terraces to the River Boyne. The tower of a small church, built in 1807, rises a few hundred feet from the house near the old kitchen garden, which itself is graced both by a conservatory and a summerhouse. So when Mrs. Waddington inherited Beaulieu she also inherited several interesting buildings to provide focal points for her garden.

Wisely, she chose not to develop the garden around her architecturally distinguished house, for which the green of the limes provides the best foil. Rather, the old kitchen garden was her point of departure. The traditional Irish kitchen garden is typically devoted to fruit and vegetables along the sides, with flower borders running down its center. The plan at Beaulieu, however, is different, for the sloping ground has led to the creation of two levels, the upper one being the flower garden, the lower the vegetable and fruit garden. The flower borders run the length of the upper terrace, accenting at one end the conservatory and at the other the summerhouse. It was bold of Mrs. Waddington to keep the very long borders as they were, without breaking them up into smaller units. She has made one change, however. Before her time, the central gravel path was as straight as a die—adhering to the strict, calculated discipline admired by the Victorians in gardening as in other walks of life. Mrs. Waddington has followed today's more relaxed approach, planting dwarf shrubs and herbs to spill over the path from either side so that it now appears to run irregularly from one end to the other. This planting has been so successful that from some angles the path seems to disappear in a field of solid color.

For many years it was fashionable to like only white or pastel-colored flowers; arbiters of garden taste like Russell Page found bright or deep color just a little vulgar. It was not always so—witness the watercolors of gardens painted by Beatrice

Parsons and Mildred Butler some fifty years ago. Now the pendulum has swung back. People are no longer afraid to use bright color and the borders of Beaulieu are today considered well mannered.

They are designed to reach their peak in July and August. This is welcome, since most Irish gardens are at their best in the spring. Interwoven with their green foliage is a strong thread of purple, with a fennel (*Foeniculum vulgare* 'Purpureum'), a dwarf barberry (*Berberis thunbergii* 'Atropurpurea'), purple Australian flax, and the purple globe flowers of *Allium christophii*—which, together with *Allium cernuum,* seed themselves generously wherever space is available. And a purple *Rodgersia pinnata* provides a tinted base for a sundial halfway down one of the borders.

Hotly contrasted with the purples are red-hot pokers (*Kriphofia*) and the *ligtu* hybrids of alstroemeria, which flower in shades of pink, orange, and flame. Scarlets and crimsons are also woven into the tapestry. There are groups of *Monarda didyma* 'Cambridge Scarlet', bold drifts of *Lobelia tupa*, penstemons, and broad masses of phlox, of which Mrs. Waddington makes a great speciality as they reach their peak of flowering in summer. The pale pinks of *Chrysanthemum coccineum*, 'Roseum' foxgloves, and hardy geraniums strike softer notes that are enriched by the pale yellow of golden marjoram, double bachelor's buttons, and golden euonymus. Blue delphiniums contrast with flat yarrow heads. Plume poppies stand tall.

*A tapestry of plants in the golden border: from left at the back are* Cupressus macrocarpa *'Lutea'*, Chamaecyparis pisifera *'Filifera Aurea'*, Thuja occidentalis *'Lutea'*, Elaeagnus pungens *'Maculata'*, *and* Elaeagnus pungens *'Dicksonii'*. *In front is a selection of variegated euonymus.*

*Right:*
*A box garden planted with roses for cutting underplanted with violas and snapdragons and backed by black-green Irish yews is a time-honored feature of the Irish walled garden.*

*Opposite page:*
*A cottage-style planting in which the tall pink-flowering Indian balsam* Impatiens glandulifera *is allowed to wander into the purple globe flowers of* Allium christophii *and yellow heliopsis into the pink feverfew,* Chrysanthemum coccineum *'E. M. Robinson'.*

White heathers and foxgloves make a quieter contribution, and red, white, and pink valerians scramble through the crevices to flower on the red brick wall behind.

Toward the summerhouse end of the borders, on the side nearer the church, is a small box garden with a pattern of diamonds set in squares, backed by inky-black Irish yews—a time-honored combination in Irish kitchen gardens. The box pattern is inset with roses for cutting, underplanted, as is the custom, with violas and snapdragons. Mrs. Waddington has, however, reserved two of the beds for an original planting: one has been filled with peat to grow azaleas and heathers, and another is planted out in summer with the cherry pie known as *Heliotropium x hybrida* 'Marina'. Its dark purplish-gray leaves and deep violet-blue flowers look as if they are lit by moonlight.

In the conservatory grow bougainvillea, oleanders, plumbago, and daturas to remind Mrs. Waddington of the gardens in the south of France that she and her husband frequently visit.

Many gardens in this book have been made by one man or woman. That at Beaulieu, by contrast, has been made by generations of women for whom work in the flower garden has been part of the tradition of country-house living. Mrs. Waddington learned her gardening from her mother, and she in turn has passed on her enthusiasm and knowledge to her daughter. It is this sense of continuity that contributes so vitally to the charm of Beaulieu.

*The Gardens of Ireland*

# Ballymaglasson

· · · · · · · · · · · · · · · · · · · · ·

## COUNTY MEATH
### Mr. and Mrs. John Corcoran

Ballymaglasson is a stud farm. Its garden is just six years old, the youngest in this book. Both the house and the garden were designed by the author in collaboration with the owners when they decided to move closer to Dublin from County Wexford, where they had maintained a good garden for many years.

The previous house on the site had burned down. Though no garden remained, its woods and groves of trees survived to make a mature setting for the new house, which was built in a simple Georgian style. County Meath being one of the flattest counties in Ireland, one must take advantage of any slight elevation or rise in the ground. So, like the old house, the new one is sited on a hill and enjoys, on a clear day,

A gateway in the walled garden frames a view
of the horses in the fields, with hedgerows and
trees beyond.

Preceding pages:
Purple and silver foliage enhance the pinky-
gray color of the brickwork. The dark purple
tints of clematis foliage on the pillar and of
the plum tree are lightened by proximity to
the silver foliage of the weeping silver pear
and the cotton lavender, and by the white-
flowering rose 'Iceberg'.

The garden was placed to one side of the
house so as not to detract from the landscape
view in front.

views to the Dublin Mountains, twenty miles to the south. The front windows
overlook the succession of fields, hedgerows, and trees that make up the stud farm
of Ballymaglasson. So as not to detract from this pastoral view, the garden was
placed to one side of the house, but the problem of how to separate the house from
the fields remained. The owners suggested a stud fence, but its rails would have
interrupted the view. The author suggested a sunk fence, but this would have held
danger for the bloodstock. It was the late Russell Page, the eminent garden designer, who proposed the solution in 1983, and it was quickly realized: a retaining
wall, invisible from the house but forming a substantial barrier from the field. The
wall is flanked on either side by four pyramidal hornbeams, also suggested by Mr.
Page, that cleverly frame the views to and from the house.

In starting the new garden, the owners were concerned that it should remain
compact and manageable. So it was suggested that it should be contained within
walls. The walls would act as a brake on the territorial expansion that is inevitable
when a keen gardener sees and then covets more and more plants as the years go
by. But the high walls of a traditional Irish walled garden would have hidden the
view of the garden from the house, so we hit upon the idea of a garden surrounded
by dwarf walls. The site was already suggested by a nearby hedged field, sloping to
the south, where a kitchen garden had sheltered in the past. Its hedges would
provide immediate shelter and could be removed when the new protective plantings had matured. Behind was an old avenue of beech trees, planted on line with
the tower of a nearby church, that would give a mature background and height to

the new garden. More important, by linking the house, tower, beech avenue, and new garden together, we could create a sequence of interesting garden spaces.

The oval forecourt in front of the house is enclosed by shallow banks of low conifers and Saint John's Wort (hypericum) and leads into the beech avenue. The dappled shade of the avenue is lit in spring by thousands of daffodils in the grass, which lead the eye down to a circular colonnade at the opposite end. Halfway down, an opening in the trees reveals a broad grass terrace and, below it, the new walled garden. The terrace is edged with a low, loose hedge of the rose 'The Fairy'.

Steps lead down between tall pillars into the walled garden, in which a large rectangle of lawn, outlined with paving stones, is surrounded by deep mixed borders. On the opposite side, the rectangle opens into a broad bow where an opening between a matching pair of tall pillars discloses a view of the fields.

Each corner and entrance to the garden is marked by matching pillars, and the height of the surrounding walls, elsewhere only two feet, is raised to eight feet at chosen focal points, where the wall also acts as host for a series of climbing plants. The permanent foundation planting was put in first—pairs of Irish yews to frame the corner pillars, pairs of purple plums and Norway maples to mark the entrances, pairs of dwarf mountain pines and Savin junipers to mark the points where the borders change direction, and yuccas to give definition to the corners. These long-lived formal plantings provide a basic structure within which four more colorful zones of mixed shrub, bulb, and herbaceous plants have been established. Each zone has its own distinct color scheme—red, yellow, white, or purple.

*A circular lily pool fringed with water buttercup draws the eye to the wide flight of steps leading to the upper terrace and the beech walk beyond.*

*A pool of the deep scarlet flowers of* Lobelia cardinalis *'Dark Crusader' is edged with an equally vivid rock rose that spills onto the paving. Behind, the flowers of the floribunda rose 'Evelyn Fison', bred by Sam McGredy in Northern Ireland, begin to open. On the left the sensational cream-splashed poplar,* Populus candicans *'Aurora', hides the tennis court from view.*

The white border is focused on a weeping silver pear growing out of a mat of silvery lavender, cotton lavender, and stachys flanked by white potentillas and *Rubus x tridel* 'Benenden'. A clump of the floribunda rose 'Iceberg' provides a continuous sheet of white summer flowers, but more interesting for the plantsman are a young *Drimys winteri*, whose ivory-colored flowers open in May; a tall *Eucryphia* 'Nymansay', whose white flowers appear in August and September; the Californian *Romneya coulteri*, with its white, poppylike flowers from July to October; and *Cistus laurifolius*, also white, blooming from midsummer onwards. All are considered tender for inland County Meath but succeed here.

The purple borders are dominated by the glossy foliage of *Acer planatoides* 'Crimson King', two trees of which are pruned to keep their stature small and their leaves large. Below them, blue lavenders, the blue carpeting juniper *Juniperus horizontalis* 'Wiltonii', and purple-flowering *Salvia x superba* make a thick, weed-suppressing ground cover. A group of the hybrid tea rose 'Blue Moon' is a pool of silvery lilac when in flower. Behind it, an impressive *Corynabutilon vitifolium* 'Veronica Tennant' is covered with blue-mauve flowers from May to June, and the violet-blue blooms of a nearby *Hibiscus syriacus* follow. Blue ceanothus and the purple-splashed leaves of *Actinidia kolomikta* scale the wall behind.

The yellow border has the deep, rich colors of the roses 'Allgold', 'Arthur Bell', and 'Peace' at its heart. They are softened by the rings of yellow-flowering potentillas, helianthemums, mimulus, and cytisus (brooms) that surround them. Small trees with flowers and foliage of a softer yellow or gold link them to the green trees

behind. Among these are the tender Moroccan broom, *Cytisus battandieri*, with pineapple-scented flowers in June; *Sophora microphylla*, with hanging bells of mustard yellow in the same month; and *Pittosporum tenuifolium* 'Warnham Gold', with yellow leaves throughout the year. Their success in a cold, noncoastal climate justifies the original choice of such a sheltered site for the garden.

The red zone is deeply colored by the foliage of a purple plum, dwarf purple barberry, dwarf purple Japanese maples, and the red young leaves of *Photinia* 'Red Robin'. Brightening the color scheme are the crimson flowers of the roses 'Papa Meilland' and 'National Trust', which link the dark purples to the vivid red of the floribunda rose 'Evelyn Fison'. The red flowers of *Potentilla* 'Red Ace' in June are succeeded by the reds of penstemons, fuchsias, and Cape figwort in July and August. The purple foliage of the shrubs is echoed in the carpet of bugle.

Compactness in a garden is often difficult to maintain. With a formal design like that of the garden at Ballymaglasson, discipline, or a semblance of it, may be preserved. This does not preclude experimentation with plants, for, as we have seen here, the microclimate on this southern slope sheltered by beech trees has enabled the growth of numerous plants normally regarded as not hardy enough for County Meath. Also unexpected is the thriving *Nothofagus dombeyi*, normally thought to be unsuitable for growing on the limestone soil of this area. The garden at Ballymaglasson, where a formality of design coexists with an informality of planting, is thus very much in the tradition of twentieth-century garden design.

*The yellow border contains the hybrid tea rose 'Peace' and the paler yellow floribunda rose 'Allgold'.*

*The white-splashed leaves of* Hosta undulata *are highlighted against purple Japanese maples.*

# Mount Stewart

• • • • • • • • • • • • • • • • • • • • • • • •

COUNTY DOWN
The National Trust

It is a distinct advantage to be able to design a garden around a house of historic and architectural importance. Add to that a setting of mature trees and a view of a picturesque lough and you have the promising situation that greeted Edith, Lady Londonderry, when, in 1921, she and her husband, the seventh marquess of Londonderry, moved to his Irish home at Mount Stewart in County Down and began to make a garden.

The estate, situated on the Ards peninsula on the shores of Strangford Lough, had been acquired by the Stewart family in 1744. At that time, like so many Irish demesnes, the setting of the house was mainly parkland. In the mid-nineteenth century greater attention was given to the

A view from the house into the sunk garden and the shamrock garden beyond.

*Preceding pages:*
*Looking from the Spanish garden to the south front of the house designed in the 1830s by the Irish architect William Vitruvius Morrison.*

*The entrance to the shamrock garden. The Red Hand, emblem of Ulster, is etched with a close planting of the red-leaved* Iresine herbstii *in the paving, itself designed in the shape of an Irish shamrock. An Irish harp is cut in yew at the back.*

*Opposite page:*
*In the sunk garden, beds outlined with hedges of sweet bay,* Laurus nobilis, *are planted in a rich color scheme — yellow and orange day lilies and yellow mulleins contrast with purple and mauve hollyhocks, campanulas, and thalictrums.*

grounds near the house, which had itself been much enlarged in the 1830s; lawns were cleared, the coniferous trees that are now such a magnificent feature were planted, and the artificial lake was created.

The plantings had become overgrown. Lady Londonderry remembered the place as she first saw it: a house in the dark gray local stone, overshadowed by sombre evergreen oaks that almost touched the window panes . . . "the darkest, dampest, saddest place" she had ever stayed in. Perhaps it was in reaction to this first impression that she determined to infuse Mount Stewart with the lighter atmosphere of the Mediterranean by creating gardens in the Italian and Spanish styles.

Her husband, who had until then worked in London, was asked to return to Ireland to take up a cabinet post in the newly formed government of Northern Ireland in 1922. After the First World War, Ulster landlords had been asked to provide as much employment as possible for ex-service men. The Londonderrys had twenty in their employ, and it was with this band of men that Lady Londonderry, in a formidable burst of energy between 1919, when the initial clearance was begun, and 1927, when the family burial ground was complete, created the underlying structure of the garden of today. The record of activity speaks for itself. The Italian and sunk gardens were begun in 1920, the Spanish and Mairi gardens in 1923, the shamrock garden in 1924, the dodo terrace in 1925, and Tir Nan Og, the

*The Gardens of Ireland*

burial ground, in 1926. A host of peripheral planting and other development was taking place at the same time. Besides the twenty ex-service men, Lady Londonderry was assisted by her head gardener, Thomas Bolas (who retired in 1949), John Girvan, a local stonemason who built all the walls, and Thomas Beattie, who cast the balustrading and statuary. Allied to this array of craftsmanship and labor were the design skills of Miss Gertrude Jekyll, who devised the sunk garden, and Sir John Ross of Bladensburg and Sir Herbert Maxwell, who advised on planting. Lady Londonderry had assembled a team of exemplary balance and expertise.

The garden design around the house comprises two suites of formal gardens, one stretching out from the south front of the house, and the second from the west front. Around them, and separating them, are informal groves of trees and shrubs.

Lady Londonderry had already arranged for the clearing and leveling of the site of the Italian garden before her arrival at Mount Stewart in 1922. Having determined on the Italian theme, she pored over books on Italian gardens, looking for ideas. From the Boboli Gardens in Florence she chose the idea of paired columns with heraldic griffins on top. From the Villa Gamberaia, at Settignano, she chose as a model the terrace balustrading. From the Villa Farnese at Caprarola, she chose the idea of herms surrounding the garden.

She did not, however, choose an Italian model for the design of the beds in the parterre at the center, but a Scottish one—that of the garden of her mother's home,

*The sunk garden, designed by Gertrude Jekyll, is enclosed by a cypress hedge, a stone-and-timber pergola, and long borders of vivid orange azaleas.*

*The Gardens of Ireland*

*Plantings in the west parterre bed.*

*Preceding pages:*
*Looking over the Italian garden to the*
*Spanish garden and Strangford Lough*
*beyond. The parterre beds now contain a*
*mixed planting, that on the left in a strong*
*color scheme of red, yellow, and purple, that*
*on the right in a softer scheme of pink, gray,*
*and mauve.*

Dunrobin Castle. She completed the layout with an avenue of Australian cabbage palms down the center. Lady Londonderry was never a purist in design.

In 1920, the two parterre beds on the south front were planted with roses and edged with white heather. These were not a success, their cultural requirements being different—roses needing a heavy clay soil, heathers a light sandy one. In 1926 the beds were replanted with herbaceous plants and edged with a mixture of dwarf shrubs and foliage plants, all for late-summer effect. The parterre beds to the east are now mainly devoted to orange, red, and other strong colors, those to the west to softer tones of pink, gray, and mauve.

For the terrace above, fully grown clipped bay trees were imported from Ghent, Belgium, in 1923, along with a variety of tender and rare plants. Lady Londonderry's early interest in horticulture is shown by her choice of plants for this area. *Beschorneria yuccoides* from Mexico went in in 1922, as did *Feijoa sellowiana* from Brazil. *Carpenteria californica* from California was planted in 1923 and *Camellia reticulata* 'Captain Rawes' from China in 1924.

Steps lead down from the parterre to the Spanish garden, which was begun a few years later. From the Moorish gardens of the Generalife and the Alhambra in southern Spain, Lady Londonderry derived the ideas of the water tank and rills sunken in tessellated paving, the arcaded cypress hedges, the oil jars, the shady loggia, and the roof tile, but the glazed wall tiles came from Arab Palestine rather than Arab Spain. The Spanish theme is continued in the planting—variegated yuccas and dwarf fan palms (*Chamaerops humilis arborescens*), a native of Spain and the only palm native to Europe. The shape of the sunken portion of the Spanish garden is based on the design of a decorative plaster ceiling—not, however, one in some Spanish house, but one in the upper room of the Temple of the Winds, an exquisite eighteenth-century banqueting house in the park of Mount Stewart. Lady Londonderry was rarely consistent.

On either side of this suite of gardens rise tall trees of the Tasmanian blue gum (*Eucalyptus globulus*), grown from seeds brought back from South Africa by Theresa, Lady Londonderry in 1894. About a hundred feet high, they give an exotic skyline to the ensemble.

To one side of the Italian garden double steps lead up to what is known as the dodo terrace: on its balustrades is a wide assembly of cast-concrete animals, both real and fanciful—griffins, cats, horses, hedgehogs, squirrels, rabbits, and crocodiles. Lady Londonderry never lost her childlike wonder at the natural world and its animals, and throughout her life wrote children's fairy stories in which mythical creatures and beasts played a large role. The dodo terrace was to become a place for her children to experience this fantastical realm. Lady Londonderry's world of fancy and her husband's of politics coalesced in the decoration of this terrace, where many of the animals were given the faces of the Marquess's political associates during the Great War, who were known collectively as the Ark Club. A Noah's Ark in cast concrete presides at the center of the terrace, which is redolent of lavender and rosemary and graced by the magnificent foliage shrub *Melianthus major*. Nearby a Chinese wisteria clambers up the lofty trunk of a eucalyptus.

Behind the terrace is the garden known as the Mairi garden after Lady Mairi Vane-Tempest-Stewart, the youngest daughter of the house, who was placed here in her perambulator days. A lead figure of Lady Mairi, sculpted by Margaret Wrightsman, is at the center of a pool and beds in the shape of a Tudor rose. Around the pool base the nursery rhyme "Mairi, mairi, quite contrary" has been set in cockleshells. "Silver bells" are illustrated by white campanulas and "pretty

maids" by *Saxifraga granulata* 'Flore Pleno'. To one side is a shady summerhouse designed by Lady Mairi's elder sister, Lady Margaret. It is a delightful child's garden. The planting is in blue and white. The white Bourbon rose 'Boule de Neige', the white clematis *C. fargesii soulei*, the white *Buddleia fallowiana alba*, and a white fuchsia contribute to the theme.

The Mairi garden rounds off the suite of gardens leading from the south front of the house. Separating these gardens from the formal gardens on the west front is the lily wood, its dappled shade contrasting with the bright open setting of the gardens. The wood is mainly composed of Australasian, South American, and Himalayan trees and shrubs. Rare conifers like the celery pine (*Phyllocladus trichomanoides*) and the toatoa (*Phyllocladus glaucus*), both from New Zealand, and the Tasmanian cedar (*Athrotaxis selaginoides*) preside. An underlayer is provided by, among others, the Chilean *Gevuina avellana*; *Myrtus luma*; the New Zealand tree fern (*Dicksonia antarctica*); rhododendrons and cornus from the Himalayas; and a variety of very tall eucalyptus. The wood is a rich mixture, indeed, of exotic plants that provide the light cool shade in which the groups of lilies thrive. Through a gate copied from the illustration in a book by Kate Greenaway the sunk garden and the west front of the house are reached.

The sunk garden was designed by Gertrude Jekyll, whose drawings for it are in the library of the University of California at Berkeley. The large square area is

*The parterre beds on the eastern side of the Italian garden are in a color scheme of yellow and orange with hedges in complementary colors. The pool is edged with* Iris laevigata *'Rose Queen' and* Hosta plantaginea *'Grandiflora'.*

*The Gardens of Ireland*

enclosed by a tall Leyland cypress hedge, inside which a stone-and-timber pergola extends on three sides. It is decorated with roses, mainly yellow, such as 'Climbing Lady Hillingdon', 'Mermaid', 'Lawrence Johnston', and 'Easlea's Golden Rambler'. Clematis and ceanothus in variety add blue and purple to the overall coloring. Along the retaining walls yellow tree lupins, blue lithospermum, and purple violas continue the yellow, blue, and purple theme. Vivid orange is added by the long borders of the Ghent azalea 'Coccinea Speciosa' planted in 1923 above the central sunken area. Scalloped hedges of sweet bay (*Laurus nobilis*) outline the four beds on the sunken lawn. These beds contain a mixture of herbaceous plants and bulbs, blue delphiniums and orange lilies in particular, and purple clematis growing over fragrant tree heaths. In each of the four corners is a purple Norway maple (*Acer platanoides* 'Crimson King'), its hot leaf color intensifying the color scheme. The success of this garden relies on the tension between the vibrant colors of the plants, the severe geometry of the borders, and the cool green of the lawn. It is the only one of the formal gardens in which Lady Londonderry kept the design and planting under strict control, so there is a sense of restraint that is missing from the other more eclectic gardens.

An opening leads into the shamrock garden, the second of the suite on the west side. Its design is based on a variety of Irish emblems. Its plan is that of a shamrock. At its center is a bed in the paving shaped like a hand, filled with red plants

*The arcaded cypress hedges, the oil jars, the water tank and rills, and the shady loggia of the Spanish garden were derived from the Moorish gardens of the Alhambra and the Generalife in southern Spain.*

*Opposite page:*
*Behind the Dodo terrace are specimens of the magnificent Tasmanian blue gum,*
Eucalyptus globulus, *grown from seed brought back by Theresa, Lady Londonderry, from South Africa in 1894.*

*Thomas Beattie, a local craftsman, cast all the statuary in concrete, including these herms based on those in the secret garden at the Villa Farnese at Caprarola.*

to represent The Red Hand, the symbol of the ancient province of Ulster. An Irish harp, cut in yew, completes the Irish emblems; but Lady Londonderry, as in all her gardens, could not resist adding a motif from a contrasting culture. In this case, it is a set of topiary animals based on those in the psalter of Queen Mary Tudor. Originally the theme of The Red Hand was taken up in the planting, which was all in red. The point of this was lost, however, when it was replanted with winter-flowering shrubs in 1950.

The vista is continued by a memorial glade planted by Lady Mairi Bury in memory of her mother, soon after the latter's death in 1959. The planting consists of an irregular avenue of the Chilean fire bush (*Embothrium coccineum*) augmented by orange-cupped narcissus, yellow azaleas, white lilacs, blue hydrangeas, and Sargent cherry for autumn color.

Across the main drive and through rhododendron plantings (which include many *arboreum* hybrids, some achieving forty feet in height, and a large group of *R. macabeanum*, thirty feet high), a path winds out of sight of the house to the lake dug by the third marquess of Londonderry in 1846–48. Its banks and the slopes around them were cleared and planted by Lady Londonderry with large groups of flowering trees and shrubs alternating with open stretches of lawn. The open areas allowed access to the lakeside and a quiet green foil for the color in the beds. The principal groups consist of *Rhododendron arboreum* hybrids and purple Japanese maples and filberts. Their vibrant color is reflected in the lake's surface and contrasted with the cool blues of the surrounding pines.

Behind the lake the ground rises through thick plantings to what at first appears to be a folly on a hill. In fact, the tower is the two-storyed gateway to the family burial ground constructed by Lady Londonderry in 1926. It is called in Irish *Tir Nan Og*, "The Land of the Ever Young." In the corners of the garden are twin circular pavilions with colored stained glass windows. Smaller entrance gateways with ironwork in Art Deco style are flanked by niches in which shelter figures of the Irish saints Patrick and Brigid. Decorative paving, stone water channels, and earthenware pots also contribute to the interest of the setting. Beds are planted with the rose 'Fellenburg' and flanked by cypresses.

The slope below the burial ground faces south and is the warmest in the garden. Here the most tender plants grow. Lady Londonderry wrote: "The really exciting and important thing about Mount Stewart was discovering the climate, and this I think I may have claimed to have done: making the gardens around the house was the second step." She was fortunate to have as advisor on tender and half-hardy plants her neighbor, Sir John Ross of Bladensburg, who in 1920 had the largest private collection of plants in the country, and the Scotsman Sir Herbert Maxwell, author of a book on Scottish gardens. They "incited" her, she wrote, to take maximum advantage of the mild climate to grow outside a host of plants that would normally be grown only in a greenhouse. After fifty years, the fantastic size of the eucalyptus, olearias, palms, and mimosas proves the excellence of the advice of these two men. In addition a fruiting olive tree grown from seed collected in Jerusalem in 1928, a camphor tree (*Cinnamomum camphora*), one of the few in Ireland known to the author, and clumps of echiums testify to the almost Mediterranean-like climate of this garden.

From the bottom of this slope, long rides lead off into the surrounding woodland. The Jubilee walk (1935) is planted in a color scheme of red, white, and blue flowers. The ladies' walk has many rhododendrons of the tender series, of the large leaved species, and of late-flowering red species, and many smaller-leaved

species and cultivars. One ride eventually reaches a promontory overlooking the lough. Here stands James "Athenian" Stuart's Temple of the Winds built in 1785 and modelled on the famous building of classical Greece.

The garden was given to the National Trust in 1957, two years before Lady Londonderry's death. It had been thirty years in the making. The vigor—mental and physical—and the resources required to carry out such an enormous garden scheme are now seldom seen. It is thus all the more vital that the National Trust continue conserving this remarkable work of one woman's imagination.

For many years the garden has received the very personal attentions of Graham Stuart Thomas, the recently retired gardens advisor to the National Trust. Since about 1970, he has been carefully bringing the garden back to its original heights. He has given particular attention to the collections of old roses and herbaceous plants. Lady Londonderry's rose, called for her 'Dame Edith Helen,' grows once more in the Italian garden.

Nowadays as one visits gardens that are maintained, for one reason or another, at a lesser level of excellence than formerly, it is easy to forget what superb maintenance is. When one comes across it occasionally again, it comes as a pleasant shock. Such a shock awaits visitors to Mount Stewart, where outstanding maintenance, under the direction of the head gardener, Neil Marshall, allows the garden to rank again among the most notable in Europe.

*To the north of the house, Edith, Lady Londonderry, planted large groups of flowering trees and shrubs around the lake, which was dug about 1846–48. Above it is Tir Nan Og, the family burial ground, one of the towers of which can be seen at left.*

The Gardens of Ireland

# Glenveagh Castle

· · · · · · · · · · · · · · · · · · · · · · · · ·

COUNTY DONEGAL
The National Parks and Monuments Service of the
Office of Public Works

No garden is as enthralling as one in which botanical knowledge has been refined by artistic sense. Such a garden is Glenveagh Castle, set down in a remote, bleak wilderness in Donegal in the northwest corner of Ireland. The Derryveagh mountains, which enclose it, are seen by an evanescent light. Only low-growing heather and furze survive on the thin, acid mountain soil. In sheltered gullies, groves of stunted native oak (*Quercus petraea*) find some protection from the wind off the Atlantic, which brings racing clouds and shadows quickly passing over the landscape. Turning up one of the many trough-shaped glens and along by the shore of a wind-ruffled ribbon lough, one comes un-

Soil was carted down from the upper valley to level the lawn in the Pleasure Grounds. Around the lawn are groups of large-leaved and fragrant rhododendrons edged with herbaceous plantings for summer color and texture.

Preceding pages:
Paths through the woodland garden are carved out of, and built into, the sharp gray limestone rock.

Groves of sheltering Austrian and Scots pine were planted around the castle, their sombre tints offsetting the lighter green of native oak and the white flowers of native hawthorn.

expectedly upon the granite castle of Glenveagh, snugly wrapped in its sheltering pines.

The Victorian passion for deer stalking seems to have been the motive behind the formation, in the late 1850s, of this 22,000-acre estate. The owner, J. G. Adair, was an Irishman of Scottish descent, with extensive American interests. The building of the castle followed a decade later and coincided with Adair's marriage in 1867 in Paris to Cornelia Ritchie, the widowed daughter of James S. Wadsworth, a hero of the American Civil War. Adair's cousin, the architect I. T. Trench, may have suggested building a reproduction Irish medieval tower house instead of the conventional shooting lodge. The site, a promontory jutting into Lough Veagh, was chosen carefully to give sweeping views up and down the glen.

The Adairs planted the groves of sheltering Austrian and Scots pine around the castle, their sombre tints offsetting the lighter green of the native oak and the glistening hues of *Rhododendron ponticum*, tinted mauve when in flower. So began, one hundred years ago, the transformation of a barren, boggy hillside sloping down to the newly built castle on the windswept shore of Lough Veagh, into the garden we see today.

In a sheltered defile to the east of the castle, Mrs. Adair made a garden, known in Victorian parlance as the "Pleasure Grounds" (to distinguish it from the kitchen garden, for which the title "the garden" was then often exclusively reserved). To

make the level lawn on ground that was everywhere sloping and only thinly covered with soil, Mrs. Adair had additional soil carted down from the upper part of the valley. Around the new lawn Mrs. Adair planted many rhododendrons, including the giant *Rhododendron falconeri* and *sinogrande* that preside over the area today. Mrs. Adair also constructed drives to two lookout points above the castle. She would repair to these in her pony-and-trap on a warm summer's day, and they are still known as Mrs. Adair's Seats.

In 1929, the American connection was strengthened by the sale of the estate to Professor and Mrs. A. Kingsley Porter. Professor Porter was a distinguished archaeologist and professor of fine arts at Harvard University but not an enthusiastic gardener, so there was a lull in horticultural development at Glenveagh. In 1937, Mrs. Porter sold the estate to Mr. Henry McIlhenny of Philadelphia, whose grandfather had emigrated to the United States from Milford, a village nearby.

Mr. McIlhenny, whose residence in Rittenhouse Square in Philadelphia houses his famous collection of French Impressionists, was curator of decorative arts at the Philadelphia Museum of Art from 1935 until 1964 and is now chairman of the board of trustees. He is also a keen gardener. After the war he began a long and intensive period of development to bring the garden at Glenveagh to its present splendor.

He first asked the advice of James Russell, the distinguished English garden

*A single flight of stone steps leads up the steep hillside behind the castle to a high viewing point from which the gardens and woods in their loughside setting can be admired.*

*The scarlet young foliage of* Pieris formosa forrestii *creates a backdrop for stone herms in the paved garden in the woodland.*

*Opposite page:*
*Bold foliage contrasts in the Pleasure Grounds. Feathery bamboo,* Arundinaria nitida, *is a foil for the purple barberry,* Berberis thunbergii *'Atropurpurea', its bronze tints echoed in the large leaves of* Rodgersia pinnata *'Superba'.*

designer, who advised the expansion of Mrs. Adair's rhododendron collection in the Pleasure Grounds. As in music, a garden composition requires a theme. For the rhododendron plantings, two themes were chosen. First, big rhododendrons were planted, their gigantic leaves providing noble architectural form. Groups of *Rhododendron macabeanum, sinogrande,* and *falconeri,* for example, now provide strong focal points under the trees. Second, scented rhododendrons were planted. These are often tender and to be seen only in greenhouses or in gardens with a mild microclimate like Glenveagh. Now the air is scented with rhododendrons of the *maddenii* series, named after the Irishman Major Edward Madden, together with *R.* 'Polar Bear', 'Lady Alice Fitzwilliam', *lindleyii,* and *taggianum,* many of them chosen with the advice of the garden consultant Lanning Roper. *Rhododendron ciliatum,* another scented one, is unmolested by the deer and so seeds itself extensively in the damp moss, increasing by the hundred each year.

Since most rhododendrons flower in late spring or early summer, while Mr. McIlhenny came to Glenveagh only in the summer, great care was taken to provide Glenveagh with a range of plants that create interest throughout the season. Striking plants of the tree fern, *Dicksonia antarctica,* the Chusan palm, *Trachycarpus fortunei,* the outstanding *Trochodendron aralioides,* and the remarkable *Pseudopanax crassifolius* provide focal points amid the surrounding flower color. The irregular green lawn is fringed with the bold foliage of long drifts of hostas, rodgersias, and bergenias, and with the bright color of candelabra primulas and Himalayan poppies in spring, and astilbes and agapanthus in summer. The deep purple of Japanese maples provides an odd, recessive color key, and one steep slope is silvery with senecio. Lilies, which constitute another of the planting themes at Glenveagh, lay their heavy fragrance on the summer air. Its richness of planting and spatial arrangement make the Pleasure Grounds perhaps the most successful of the many gardens at Glenveagh.

Running through the wood above the Pleasure Grounds is the Belgian Walk, so called because it was constructed by Belgian soldiers convalescing at Glenveagh during the First World War. Mr. McIlhenny had clearings made from time to time along its length, letting the light in, in one case, on a newly constructed pool, in another on a drift of blue poppies, and in yet another on a break of autumn-coloring fothergilla. Many years later, in 1966, he added a surprise—a formal terrace paved with slate and furnished with Regency iron seats, huge Sicilian oil jars dated 1842, and superb stone statuary, mainly eighteenth-century Italian. Azaleas are cultivated in large earthenware pots, huge pieris and metrosideros in the surrounding beds. Italian cypresses complete the furnishing of this outdoor salon in the wilderness.

A separate series of gardens fan out along the lakeshore to the west of the castle. The Italian Garden is enclosed by hedges of griselinia inset in rhythmical arrangement with busts (imported from Florence) set on pedestals. The garden floor is of grass, its walls of rhododendron and eucryphia, and its ceiling of overhanging pines. A pair of recumbent sphinxes mark the entrance and it is furnished with stone seats and urns.

The cosmopolitan theme is continued in the Swiss Walk, laid out about 1954 and named for Mr. Brugger, the Swiss assistant to James Russell, the overall garden designer. At the end of the Swiss Walk one discovers two contrasting vistas—one closed and shaded, focusing on an urn, and the other, the View Garden, open to the lough. It is a surprise to find that this is the only garden at Glenveagh with a view of the lough. One wonders, for a moment, why the layout does not take better advantage of the surrounding scenery. But in Ireland, with its high rainfall and

*The Gardens of Ireland*

mild temperature, wind is the great enemy of gardening; plants flourish best in enclosed and sheltered spaces. At Glenveagh, the wind can suddenly, and without warning, sweep down the valley with great force, the calm lough, with equal suddenness, becoming a seething mass of waves and flying spume.

A gate from the View Garden leads out onto a heather-clad hill and into the dappled shade of an oak grove. Deep gullies, watered by rushing streams, descend the hill. The floors of the gullies are strewn with granite boulders luxuriantly clothed in moss and lichen and bedded in ferns. These natural gardens make a fine contrast with the man-made gardens within the walls. Mr. Russell had the idea of constructing a stone path up one of the gullies to enable its beauties to be explored and enjoyed more easily. Along one of its steep, rocky flanks, he constructed a precipitous flight of sixty-seven steps to reach a grass belvedere above. Huge terra-cotta pots filled with fragrant azaleas line the upper steps to remind one that this is a man-made garden, not a Cyclopean staircase or a phenomenon of nature. At the top, a terrace lawn is—breathlessly—reached. A grass bay opens out with a view of the castle, the lough, and the mountains beyond. At the far end, a hidden path leads to a thatched summerhouse set among rhododendrons. Through these a narrow peep has been cut to the castle below. It is the climax of the garden.

To unite the suites of gardens to the east and west of the castle, Mr. McIlhenny concentrated in later years on developing a walled kitchen garden, or—to use the

French term—a *potager,* to the south. It looks today as if it might have been there for centuries; in fact, the walls were built in 1957. It is entered from the castle precincts through a Gothic conservatory designed by that French chronicler of decadence, Philippe Jullian. Pale yellow mimosa, blue plumbago, passionflowers, daturas, strelitzias, and other lush exotica make this a heady place in which to sit on a summer's afternoon. Terraces on different levels, furnished with a rich assortment of seats, urns, and statuary in a mixture of many materials, are somehow successfully integrated into one design. Large earthenware pots filled with hostas and arum lilies, as they are in the gardens of Italy, are one of the recurring themes of the garden.

The *potager* extends in front of these terraces. This kitchen garden is neatly divided by gravel paths, some of which are lined with parsley and chives, others with wild strawberries, still more with gaily colored bedding plants in summer. These decorative edgings outline plots in which vegetables burgeon in neat rows, flowers for cutting bloom in blocks, and fruit ripens on sculpturally pruned trees. In the borders under the surrounding walls grow phlox and delphiniums, their strong coloring tempered by an abundant use of silver foliage, particularly celmisias with rosettes of silky leaves and white daisy flowers.

The late Russell Page, perhaps the greatest of modern garden designers, wrote in his book *The Education of a Gardener* of the difficulty of placing an artificial

*Boulder-strewn gullies, carpeted with moss and fern under a canopy of native durmast oak, descend the hillside behind the castle.*

*Opposite page:*
*The Tuscan garden is outlined by a griselinia hedge inset with a rhythmical arrangement of busts from Florence.*

*One of the busts in the Tuscan garden.*

*The Gothic conservatory behind the castle was designed by the French cultural historian Philippe Jullian. Box trees clipped into corkscrew shapes and terra-cotta pots filled with the blue hosta,* Hosta sieboldii, *furnish the terraces in the Italian manner.*

pool in front of a natural body of water, such as a lake or the sea, for the artificial color of the pool water may be badly out of key with the color of the natural water behind. Mr. McIlhenny's last project at Glenveagh was to make a swimming pool in just such a place—in front of the lake. Despite the fact that it is hidden from the castle windows and that its changing rooms and walls are turreted and battlemented, its integration provided a difficult problem, and there are differing opinions as to its success.

Over a period of forty years, Mr. McIlhenny turned the garden of Glenveagh into one of the most celebrated in Ireland. Through his lavish entertainment of his sophisticated and cosmopolitan friends in this extraordinary setting, the hospitality of Glenveagh has become legendary. The secret of the success of the gardens at Glenveagh lies in the counterpoint between the savage wilderness of the setting and the studied exquisiteness of the effects.

In 1983, the ownership of the entire property was transferred to the Irish state. The garden, it is hoped, will go on developing as part of a park under the control of the National Parks and Monuments Service, which has acquired this dramatic tract of land in order to preserve it as an amenity for the nation. The new head gardener, Mary Forrest, succeeds Matt Armour, who served as head gardener throughout Mr. McIlhenny's years at Glenveagh. Mary Forrest's first task was to make the garden ready to receive the public during the summer months. In 1985,

its first year, in a two-month period of opening, over thirty thousand people visited —and this was just the beginning. Such numbers will inevitably require alteration in a garden created for the enjoyment of a few. Already a range of new reception and administration buildings have been constructed near the entrance gates to the estate. Although they have been concealed behind enormous mounds, their red-tiled roofs and, indeed, their very presence have shattered that sense of remoteness that was once the principal characteristic of the place. A wise decision has been made, however, in barring private cars from the estate, so that once one is inside, this mountainside haunt of near a thousand red deer and this distant haven of the art of gardening can continue to give the pleasure for which it was formed.

*In Ireland wind is the great enemy of gardening. At Glenveagh, the wind can suddenly, and without warning, sweep down the lough with great force, so the gardens were made in sheltered enclosures. The Tuscan garden is seen here from the tower of the castle.*

# Gardens Open to the Public

. . . . . . . . . . . . . . . . . . . .

1
**Annes Grove**
Castletownroche, Co. Cork

2
**Bantry House**
Bantry, Co. Cork

3
**Birr Castle**
Birr, Co. Offaly

4
**Castlewellan**
Co. Down

5
**Creagh**
Skibbereen, Co. Cork

6
**Derreen**
Lauragh, near Kenmare, Co. Kerry

7
**Emo Court**
Emo, Co. Laois

8
**Fernhill**
Sandyford, Co. Dublin

9
**Fota**
Carrigtwohill, Co. Cork

10
**Glenveagh Castle**
Churchill, Co. Donegal

11
**Ilnacullin**
Garinish Island, Glengariff, Co. Cork

12
**John F. Kennedy Park**
New Ross, Co. Wexford

13
**Killruddery**
Bray, Co. Wicklow

14
**Lismore Castle**
Lismore, Co. Waterford

15
**Malahide Castle**
**Talbot Botanic Garden**
Malahide, Co. Dublin

16
**Mount Stewart**
Newtownards, Co. Down

17
**Mount Usher**
Ashford, Co. Wicklow

18
**National Botanic Garden**
Glasnevin, Dublin

19
**Powerscourt**
Enniskerry, Co. Wicklow

20
**Rowallane**
near Saintfield, Co. Down

Gardens discussed or illustrated that are open to the public. Dates and times of opening may be obtained from the leaflets published annually by the tourist boards of the Republic of Ireland and of Northern Ireland.

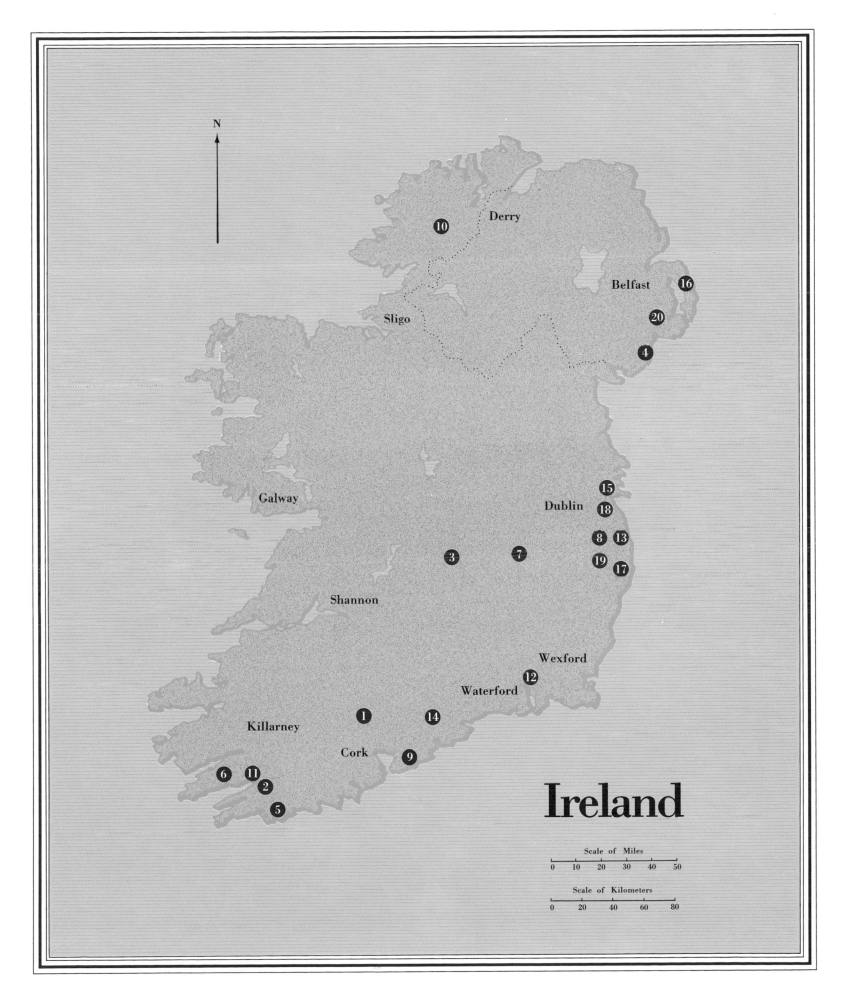

# Ireland

N

Derry

Belfast

Sligo

⑩

⑯

⑳

④

Galway

⑮

Dublin

⑱

⑧ ⑬

③

⑦

⑲

⑰

Shannon

Wexford

⑫

Waterford

Killarney

①

⑭

Cork

⑨

⑥ ⑪

②

⑤

Scale of Miles

0  10  20  30  40  50

Scale of Kilometers

0  20  40  60  80

# Horticultural Index

Italicized page numbers refer to illustrations and follow text references.

campanula, 54, 85–88, 141, 146–147, 148, 168–169, *85, 152, 164*
*Campanula* (bellflower)
    *lactiflora, 33*
    *persicifolia, 79, 147*
camphor tree (see *Cinnamomum camphora*)
carnation, 103
*Carpenteria californica*, 168
*Carrierea calycina*, 124
ceanothus, 23, 62, 97, 136, 160, 171, *10, 61, 66, 79, 96*
*Ceanothus*
    *griseus horizontalis, 62*
    *impressus, 79*
cedar, 110
    incense (see *Libocedrus decurrens*)
    Japanese (see *Cryptomeria japonica*)
    Tasmanian (see *Athrotaxis selaginoides*)
    western red (see *Thuja plicata*)
cedar of Lebanon, *62*
celery pine (see *Phyllocladus trichomanoides*)
celmisia, 181
*Chamaecyparis*
    *lawsoniana* (Lawson cypress) 'Columnaris', 79
      'Fletcheri Nana', 79
      'Intertexta Pendula', 109
      'Lutea', 140
      'Tabuliformis', 108–109
      'Triomphe de Boskoop', 140
      'Wisselii', 54
    *nootkatensis* 'Pendula' (weeping cypress), 54
    *pisifera* (Sawara cypress), *28*
      'Filifera Aurea', *154*
      'Plumosa Aurea', *81*
      'Plumosa Rogersii', *78*
      'Squarrosa', *81*
*Chamaerops humilis arborescens* (dwarf fan palm), 168
cherry, 62, 73, 84, 130, 134, 142, *23*
    Sargent, 128, 172
cherry pie (see *Heliotropium x hybrida* 'Marina')
chestnut, 21, 55, 73, *74*
chives, 181
*Chrysanthemum coccineum* 'E. M. Robinson' (feverfew), 153, *154*
*Cinnamomum camphora* (camphor tree), 42, 172
cistus, 29, 43, *32, 81*
*Cistus laurifolius*, 160
clematis, 23, 54, 56, 171, *84, 158*
*Clematis*
    *fargesii soulei*, 169
    *montana, 66, 62, 67, 192*
    *montana rubens, 62*
    *tanguica, 134*
*Clethra arborea* (lily-of-the-valley tree), 72
colchicum (autumn crocus), 73, 110
columbine, *32*
    red (see *Aquilegia coccinea*)
comfrey (see *Symphytum x uplandicum* 'Variegata')
*Cordyline australis* (cabbage palm), *40*
cornus, 169
*Cornus controversa* 'Variegata', *93*
corokia, 36
*Corokia cotoneaster* (wire netting bush), *71*
coronilla, 66
*Corynabutilon vitifolium* 'Veronica Tennant', 160
cotoneaster, 128, 130
*Cotoneaster conspicuus*, 60
    'Rothschildianus', 54
    'Santa Monica', 54
*Crambe cordifolia* (sea kale), 147
crab apple, 130
    Chinese or tea (see *Malus hupehensis*)
crimson glory vine (see *Vitis coignetiae*)
crinodendron, 48
*Crinodendron hookeranum* (lantern tree), 91
*Crocosmia masonorum* 'Lucifer', 147
crocus, 110, 130
    autumn (see colchicum)
cryptomeria, 81
*Cryptomeria japonica* (Japanese cedar), 47
    'Nana', 80–81
*Cupressus*
    *cashmeriana* (Kashmir cypress), 66, 110
    *glabra* (smooth Arizona cypress), 54
    *lusitanica* 'Glauca Pendula', 62
    *macrocarpa* (Monterey cypress), *32*, 47, 120, 128
      'Lutea', *154*
currant (see *Ribes speciosum*)
cyclamen, 62, 110

cypress, 34, 168, 172, *165, 171*
    Arizona, smooth (see *Cupressus glabra*)
    dawn (see *Metasequoia glyptostroboides*)
    Italian, 66, 178
    Kashmir (see *Cupressus cashmeriana*)
    Lawson, 23, 28, 80, 108–109, *26, 81* (see also *Chamaecyparis lawsoniana*)
    Leyland, 169–171
    Mediterranean (see Italian cypress)
    Monterey (see *Cupressus macrocarpa*)
    Sawara (see *Chamaecyparis pisifera*)
    swamp, 89
    weeping Nootka (see *Chamaecyparis nootkatensis* 'Pendula')
    Wisselii Lawson (see *Chamaecyparis lawsoniana* 'Wisselii')
cytisus, 160
*Cytisus battandieri* (Moroccan broom), 161

*Dacrydium cupressinum*, 37
daffodil, 84, 128, 134, 159
dahlia, 54
    'Bishop of Llandaff', *130*
daisy, 105, 108
*Daphniphyllum macropodum*, 42
datura, 154, 181
daylily, 23, 28, 141, 147, *164*
delphinium, 23, 56, 79, 85–88, 107, 126, 146–147, 153, 171, 181, *79, 147*
*Dendromecon rigida, 62, 60*
deutzia, 128
*Dianthus deltoides, 33*
*Dicksonia antarctica* (tree fern), 42, 48–49, 72, 92, 169, 178, *40, 41, 46*
dogwood, American, 128, *89*
dracaena (see palm, cordyline)
drimys, 36, 84
*Drimys*
    *lanceolata* ([Tasmanian mountain] pepper), 91
    *winteri*, 160

echium, 93, 172
*Ehretia dicksonii*, 128
*Elaeagnus pungens*
    'Dicksonii', *154*
    'Maculata', *154*
*Embothrium coccineum* (Chilean fire bush), 36, 54, 89, 172, *47*
*Endymion non-scriptus* (bluebell), *72*
epimedium, 128
*Eremurus bungei* (foxtail lily), 149, *149*
*Erica*
    *arborea* (tree heather), 171
    *carnea* (winter heather), *74*
*Erigeron mucronatus*, 105, 108
escallonia, 36, 62, 141
*Escallonia*
    *rubra macrantha*, 60
    'Apple Blossom', *96*
eucalyptus, 42, 72, 110, 168, 169, 172, *108*
    Australian, 14
*Eucalyptus*
    *globulus* ([Tasmanian] blue gum), 47, 48, 110, 168, 171
    *viminalis* (ribbon gum) 91, *108, 110*
eucryphia, 36, 110, 178
*Eucryphia* 'Mount Usher', 110
    'Nymansay', 160
euonymus, 153, *154*
*Euonymus fortunei* 'Silver Queen', *152*
*Euphorbia*
    *characias, 70*
    *wulfenii, 60*

*Feijoa sellowiana*, 168
fennel, purple (see *Foeniculum vulgare* 'Purpureum')
fern, 71, 74, 84, 110, 128, 180, *181*
    Killarney (see *Trichomanes speciosum*)
    tree (see *Dicksonia antarctica*)
feverfew (see *Chrysanthemum coccineum* 'E. M. Robinson')
figwort, Cape, 161
filbert, 172
fir, 107
    Caucasian (see *Abies nordmanniana*)
    Douglas (see Pseudotsuga menziesii)
fire bush, Chilean (see *Embothrium coccineum*)
*Fitzroya cupressoides*, 37

flax, 108
    Australian (see Australian flax)
*Foeniculum vulgare* 'Purpureum' (purple fennel), 152
*Fokienia hodginsii*, 37
forget-me-not, 79, *32, 126*
    Chatham Island, 36
forsythia, 136
fothergilla, 178
foxglove, 154
    'Roseum', 153
*Fremontodendron, 62, 62*
    *californicum, 62*
    *mexicanum, 62*
    'California Glory', *60, 62*
fuchsia, 10, 56, 161, 169, *52*
furze, 40, 175, *43*

*Galactites*, 97
    *tomentosa, 96*
geranium, 97, 140, 153, *93*
*Geranium*
    *argenteum, 96*
    *nigricans, 96*
*Gevuina avellana*, 169
*Ginkgo biloba* (maidenhair tree, tree of heaven), 56, *56*
gladiolus, 107
goat's beard (see *Aruncus dioicus*)
golden-rain (see *Koelreuteria bipinnata*)
gorse, 10, *10, 47*
grevillea, 36
griselinia, 178, *181*
*Griselinia littoralis, 60*
gum, blue (see *Eucalyptus globulus*)
    ribbon (manna) (see *Eucalyptus viminalis*)
gunnera, 28, 56, 66, 89, 93, 108, 141, *26, 125*
*Gunnera manicata, 48*

hakea, 62
hawthorn, *26, 176*
heath and heather, 10, 40, 43, 62, 74, 154, 168, 175, 180, *43*
    tree (see *Erica arborea*)
    winter (see *Erica carnea*)
hebe, 62, 79, 81, 96
*Hebe pinguifolia* 'Pagei', 79
*Hedera helix* 'Buttercup' (golden ivy), *93*
*Helenium autumnale* 'Moorheim Beauty' (American sneezeweed), *24*
helianthemum, 43, 81, 160
helichrysum, 80
*Helichrysum splendidum*, 135
heliopsis, *154*
*Heliotropium x hybrida* 'Marina' (cherry pie), 154
hemlock, 110
    weeping (see *Tsuga canadensis* 'Pendula')
    western (see *Tsuga heterophylla*)
*Hermodactylus tuberosus* (widow iris), 62
heuchera, 88
*Hibiscus syriacus*, 160
*Hieracium villosum*, 96
hoheria, 36, 48
holly, 72–73
hollyhock, *164*
honeysuckle (see *Lonicera chrysantha, L. sempervirens*)
hornbeam, 102, 126, 147, 158, *124*
hosta, 23, 84, 93, 109, 141, 178, 181, *40*
*Hosta*
    *plantaginea* 'Grandiflora', *169*
    *sieboldiana elegans*, 79
    *sieboldii, 28, 182*
    *undulata*, 161
hyacinth, 103
hydrangea, 28, 43, 48, 52, 54, 79, 80, 108, 110, 141, 172, *52, 79*
    climbing (see *Hydrangea petiolaris*)
*Hydrangea petiolaris*, 136
hymenophyllum, 109
hypericum (Saint John's wort), 140, *93*
*Hypericum*
    *elatum, 52*
    *ruwenzoriense, 62*

iberis, *32*
*Impatiens glandulifera* (Indian balsam), *154*
*Iresine herbstii*, 164
iris, 23, 88, 126, 142
    Japanese, 56
    water, 109

Designed by Clifford Selbert
Edited by Betty Childs
Production coordination by Christina Holz
Composition in Bodoni by Dix Type Co.Inc.
Printed in Italy by Sagdos

*Illustration page 186:*
*At Annes Grove,* Rhododendron 'Lady
Rosebery', *a hybrid of* R. cinnabarinum *bred
in 1930 by Lionel de Rothschild at Exbury,
England.*

*Preceding pages:*
*In May at Annes Grove,* Clematis montana
*rambles through* Ribes speciosum, *a
flowering currant from California.*